GRAPHIC ART
OF THE 19TH CENTURY

GRAPHIC ART
THE
19TH CENTURY

BY

CLAUDE ROGER-MARX

McGRAW-HILL

BOOK COMPANY, INC.

NEW-YORK — TORONTO — LONDON

Translated from the French by E. M. Gwyer

© 1962 EDITIONS AIMERY SOMOGY
LIBRARY OF CONGRESS CATALOG CARD NUMBER 62-20257
BOUND BY VAN RIJMENAM, N.V., THE HAGUE, HOLLAND
53418

PRINTED IN FRANCE

CONTENTS

WOOD ENGRAVING FROM 1860-1900
Page 226

INTO THE TWENTIETH CENTURY
Page 239

LIST OF ILLUSTRATIONS
Page 243

INDEX OF NAMES
Page 249

INTRODUCTION

THE ART OF ENGRAVING, so often on the point of extinction, has always in the end owed its salvation to a combination of writers and painters. During the 19th century, Théophile Gautier, followed by Baudelaire, Bracquemond, Burty, the brothers Goncourt, Buhot, Guérard, Roger-Marx, Lepère and Ambroise Vollard, managed to re-awaken enthusiasm for engraving and save the art from the monotony brought about by economic difficulties, or the mistakes perpetuated by the professionals in their teaching. Opposition between the technical specialists and the artist-engravers grew fiercer than ever: between the specialists who believed that only they held the secrets of technique and the artist-engravers who, at their very first attempts, could put the work of their instructors in the shade. On one side, the professionals; on the other, the painters or sculptors for whom engraving was neither their sole ambition nor their sole means of livelihood.

For the specialist, all that counts is his craft. But a man may know exactly how to use an etching needle, how to bite a plate, how to pull a proof and still have nothing to say. That, unhappily, has been the case with many whose technical expertise has made them despise artist-engravers as being mere prentice-hands, ignorant of style and of the rudiments of their craft. But in art, specialisation has never been noted for its results; in art, the specialist is almost always wrong.

Not that the present work is intended to be an apologia for amateur efforts; *les violons d'Ingres*, for example. The point simply is that, once a craft

7

ceases to be a new discovery, its exercise becomes automatic. The artist, like the writer, has to beware of habit which ends by killing love. Unfortunately, the public is only too apt to tie the creative artist down to a single, narrow and rigid formula. It is so convenient to be able to classify an artist and his work once for all.

Take as example any of the great masters: although his nudes and landscapes are as good as anything he ever did, Barye is known only for his animal paintings; for years, Corot's figures were sacrificed to his landscapes; for years, Daumier failed to win recognition except as a caricaturist; the public never wanted anything from Jongkind but water-colours. But to specialise in one subject leads to results as barren as those of specialising in one technique. Paradoxical as it may seem, the best war pictures are not produced by artists who have specialised in military subjects, nor the best animal studies by animal painters. Water-colourists, wood-engravers and lithographers attach all the importance they do to the little hyphen joining the words 'artist' and 'engraver' just because they realise that all that is good in their work comes from knowledge they have gained outside the practice of engraving. It comes from their knowledge of the fundamental laws that transcend this or that specific skill and that they have gradually come to understand through their painting, sculpting or drawing, because every art springs from, and is nourished by, the same great truths.

Félix Bracquemond knew this—Bracquemond who, with Théophile Gautier, Baudelaire and Burty, was one of the most persuasive champions of original engraving, as well as an admirable craftsman and up to all the tricks of the trade. His words are like a profession of faith. The true teachers of engraving have been the painters, the great masters. All that the engravers, properly so-called, have ever tried to do has been to perfect and standardise techniques the painters have discovered. No portrait engraver ever surpassed Van Dyck at linear patterns; no topographical engraver ever surpassed Canaletto or Piranesi; no landscape engraver ever tackled his work with more skill than Claude Lorrain or Ruisdael. None of these artists took up engraving for its own sake. They took it up because they wanted to plot and design their engravings in the same way as they painted their pictures.

To young artists asking advice, Bracquemond used to say: 'What does being rich mean in every-day life? It means having a fortune, possessing houses and securities. But securities are no good for paying the rent; you need bank-notes for that. Equally, bank-notes are no good for paying your bus fare for which you need small change. In art, too, try to be as rich as you can. Your real capital is emotion, sensibility, temperament. It is everything you inherit from your country, from your ancestry, your family and your epoch. It is every event and experience that has formed us and made us what we are. Our bank-notes are the knowledge we have gained of the physical world, from what we see, from our study of the sources of light, our study of values, of the laws governing colour contrasts and affinities, our study of proportion and perspective; everything Leonardo, Dürer and Cennini, to say nothing of the moderns, tell us about in their writings. Lastly comes the small change: technique in the

THOMAS ROWLANDSON. *View of London*. Hand coloured engraving

proper sense of the word, the choice of materials, pigments, oils, working tools.

'A great artist is one with a large parcel of the securities we have called temperament and a good wad of the bank-notes we have called knowledge. Finally, he also needs a little small change. A little, not too much. Rembrandt had that much inspiration (here Bracquemond would draw a circle); that much knowledge (a smaller circle, inside the first); and that much technique (a still smaller circle). As for Meissonier, he has as much technique as anyone could want but no more than a grain of inspiration. Meissonier has nothing but small change.'

At various times, in various places, schools have existed for teaching girls the arts of love. No doubt the professionals produced by these schools were selected for their natural gifts, and no doubt too they had, as Bracquemond would say, as much knowledge as anyone could want. But what is knowledge compared with temperament and real passion?

Passion, of course, is not everything, and art offers many examples of enthusiasm unaccompanied by skill. The world is full of sincere persons who will never achieve anything because they have no technique. That is what makes the critic's task so ungrateful, when faced with someone whose efforts are genuine and intentions wholly admirable but who has not the skill to express what he feels. On the other hand, real temperament rarely takes long to find its proper channel. It comes into the world armed at all points, as Delacroix said of Géricault. A couple of words of advice and it is flying alone.

The history of engraving is full of discoveries of this kind. After he had worked for the shortest possible time with Lievens, Rembrandt knew more than his teacher. After that, in a sense all he had to do was to unlearn; in other words, to re-create. His genius allowed him to break every rule.

The name of Joachim von Sandrart would be forgotten today, were it not he who taught Claude Lorrain the elements of engraving. In more modern times, Bléry the engraver taught Meryon, who never had any regular instruction, how to make his line work stand out. After a single lesson in dry point from Legros, Rodin knew how to use the point and could surpass the work of the most experienced craftsmen. Corot left it to Bracquemond to arrange for the biting of his *Tuscan* or *Italian Scenes,* and it was Bracquemond who taught Manet how to use the grain. A few words of advice from Fantin-Latour enabled Redon to discover how to revive the art of lithography. It may be doubted whether it took longer to initiate Toulouse-Lautrec into the art of lithography than it did Daumier. Coming to still more modern times, the minimum of directions from Laboureur was all that was needed by Dunoyer de Segonzac.

The present work is not intended, it need hardly be said, solely as a defence of those artists who have regarded engraving as a mere pastime and made no effort to study it seriously. But we shall see that even the greatest of those who revived different kinds of techniques, even an artist like Robert Nanteuil who did some admirable pastel work, were almost always experimenting in several directions at once.

'In the work of any of the great masters', to quote Bracquemond again, 'the artist can be seen to move further and further away from his original method. His freedom of expression becomes such that, in comparison with his earlier style, he may seem to be neglecting the rules of technique, or even throwing them away altogether. But that kind of facility is only to be gained by endless practice.'

What distinguishes the artist-engraver is that the choice of wood, copper or stone as his medium, provides him, so to speak, with his inspiration; or, to put it more accurately, the discipline imposed on him by his material turns into an additional source of strength and richness. Just as, to the true poet, rhyme and metre are a stimulus and not a hindrance, so in some mysterious way his material is a help and inspiration to the engraver.

Two-dimensional as it is and restricted to black and white, engraving, which is only one department of drawing, has nevertheless its own language and rules. Once it tries to set up as a rival to painting, it is lost. It exists in order to provide

Francisco de Goya. *Self-portrait. 1799.* Etching

FRANCISCO DE GOYA. *The Caprices: Pretty Teacher.* *1799.* Etching

a series of accepted abbreviations and transpositions; a system of 'constants' as Paul Valéry called it. The essence of engraving resides in line, how and where it is placed; but its life-blood is the ink which joins the incised lines of the plate or raised surfaces of the wood-block in a mysterious marriage with the paper. Any engraver worthy of the name knows that it is in this union of ink and paper that the peculiar beauty of his art consists. So with the true lover of engraving what he worships is the hidden life of this captured world, the movement of each stationary line, the constant interplay of light and shade. It is in this that the joy derived from the type of engraving to which this volume gives first place consists: the type of engraving characterised, according to Henri Focillon, that most admirable of critics, by its 'intensity'.

ORIGINAL COPPERPLATE AND WOOD ENGRAVING IN THE EARLY NINETEENTH CENTURY

The artist's vocation is as constant as that of the writer, namely, to evoke simultaneously the external and the internal worlds. Style and technique, however, as well as choice of theme, remain dependent on and akin to his own epoch. Even the greatest artists have to begin by submitting to certain given fashions and influences before they can acquire full freedom of expression and the power of immortalising, in their turn, new ways of feeling and seeing. This is especially true of engraving, an art whose products enjoy wide circulation and in which actual execution plays such a decisive role.

The 18th century continued to assign first place to portrait engravings, and hence to take the conventional and yet life-like portraits of Robert Nanteuil as its models. Unfortunately, it became more and more customary for engravings after original paintings or pastels to be made by professional engravers, not by the painters themselves. But in spite of this, all kinds of technical processes, many, like the mezzotint, introduced from England, enabled the engravers, if not to do away with the burin altogether, at least to mitigate its austerity by introducing certain new and lighter notes.

In France, the influence of Rubens and of the Italian school—then lately rediscovered—combined with the growing taste for nudes and *scènes galantes* to produce engravings as striking and full of life as the three-colour chalk, or pastel drawings, from which they were taken. But only very rarely would a Watteau, a Boucher or a Fragonard consent, in an idle moment, to be his own

FRANCISCO DE GOYA. *The Caprices: Till Death.* *1799.* Etching

interpreter. (Gabriel de Saint-Aubin remains an exception to this rule.) Whether for single plates or for series, painters preferred to rely on the skill and patience of the experts.

The chief beauty of Italian engraving lay in its power of evoking imaginary scenes, rather than in its delineation of detail. Hence, etching, in which the draughtsman has full freedom, offered a technique that enabled the two Tiepolos, Canaletto and Piranesi to preserve the full flow of their inspiration. These four, with Callot, Claude Lorrain and Van Dyck, may be called the fathers of the original engraving of the 19th century. Right up to the middle of the 19th century, however, by right of primogeniture, line engraving, in spite of being already then in its decline, continued to be taught in the schools and considered as the noblest, indeed the only noble, engraving technique.

Wood engraving, in which the Germans had proved themselves masters, had preceded etching, but it only survived into the 18th century in the form of book ornamentation and illustrations for almanacks and pamphlets. Anonymous, coloured in angry reds and blues, wood engraving was the prerogative of the populace, who relied on it for enforcing their claims, illustrating ballads, or giving fresh life to the old legends. In course of time, however, especially in England, etching which demanded less time than even the simplest wood engraving, became the controversialist's favourite weapon. Hogarth's *Marriage à la Mode* is the precursor of the work of Rowlandson and Cruikshank and of those who, because they exaggerated man's characteristics, would later be called caricaturists. Although the two last named were still active in the early years of the 19th century, the best part of their work really belongs to the century before. But they deserve mention nevertheless, especially Rowlandson, whose liveliness and vigour, that so captivated the young Delacroix, undoubtedly gave the impulse to the development of caricature in France, as well as influencing the work of Daumier and that of the whole team collected by Philippon—who, however, as will be seen, found a new weapon in the use of lithography.

Rowlandson (1756-1827) offers infinitely varied fare, part delicate, part coarse. Wherever he is, he finds matter for exuberant amusement. He is like a north-countryman come to town, drunk with the gin, the beer, the noise, the lights, the crowds, free with grimace and gesture, the eyes popping out of his head. His most attractive engravings, printed in black and white, are the perfect expression of his feverish excitement and it is our misfortune that those responsible for finishing them off and adding the colour should, in so many cases, have distorted the values and so spoiled drawing which can be said to burn the paper it is done on.

It was in a country not hitherto remarkable for its engraving that there suddenly appeared the greatest visionary of them all, since Rembrandt, who was to produce on copperplate a unique and prolific body of work.

Goya was fifty-three when, towards the dawn of the 19th century, he produced his first series, the *Caprices* (1799). Up to that time, his only engraved work had been a few plates done after Velásquez. His short, vigorous statements and his sparing use of line are witness to the lessons he had learned from the

Francisco de Goya. *The Disasters of War: Bury them and be silent.* *c. 1810.* Etchin

Italian etchers during his youth, above all from Tiepolo who might, indeed, be responsible for much of Goya's work, were it not that he lacks the sense of the tragic which is implicit in the earliest of Goya's original compositions, such as *The Prisoner* (I) or *The Garrotted Man.*

The *Landscape with a Great Rock, Landscape with a Waterfall* and *The Prisoner* (II) are early examples of Goya's use of aquatint combined with a light-handed technique, a method he adopted thereafter as a quick means of producing the tone effects he required.   His first masterpiece as an engraver was the *Colossus,* for which he used a smoked copper-plate much in the manner of a mezzotint.

The twenty-four plates of the *Caprices,* the title of which recalls Tiepolo, are satiric drawings of which the full implications escape us today.   Their explanation is to be found, however, in a preface inspired by Goya himself: 'In the belief that the criticism of human vices and errors can as well take the form of pictures, the author has chosen as his subjects some of the many extravagances and errors that are to be found in any civilised society.   He has selected those he

16

regards as suitable objects of ridicule and that also provide scope for the exercise of fantasy and imagination ... By selecting from the general what it considers best suited to its ends, painting, like poetry, unites in one imaginary figure circumstances and characteristics that nature has spread out over more than one. Ingenious combinations of this kind produce successful imitations which are thus made to appear original inventions and not slavish copies.'

Printed in a warm, reddish black, the series of engravings made by Goya in Madrid between the years 1793 and 1798 thus belong to the turn of the century. The instant recognition they won throughout Europe was such that forgeries began to appear almost immediately. Their success was due partly to the vehement attacks they made on the holders of power and partly to the biting force of their drawing. By following Rembrandt in his use of chiaroscuro, Goya had brought life to his forms, emphasised his contrasts and succeeded in passing, at one bound, from the seen to the imagined, from the sublime to the horrific.

Goya the diabolist never concealed his worship of Rembrandt. Despite the spiritual distance that separates these two geniuses, despite the extravagance that distinguishes the Spanish artist, it is impossible to ignore their basic similarity as instanced by their use of line and arrangement of light and shade. This similarity appears even more clearly in some of the plates of *The Disasters of War (Desastres de la Guerra)* such as *Sad presentiments of what must come to pass, Truth is Dead* and *This is the Truth*. Like *The Proverbs (Disparates)* and the twenty-four plates of *Bullfights (Tauromaquia)*, *The Disasters of War* were only published long after Goya's death; but there is no doubt of the fascination they held not only for the Romantics (Delacroix took them as the basis of several of his earlier compositions) but also for Manet, who borrowed several of his themes from them. *Exotic Flower* is a pastiche of *Good Advice (Bellos Consejos)* in *The Caprices* series. Manet also copied Goya's style of drawing, in which the background is made to stand out by the use of short, separate strokes, as well as adopting aquatint as a useful simplifying and tone process.

Except for Picasso, no painter of the 19th or the 20th century has produced so important a body of etched work as Goya. His tardy but none the less essential contribution to lithography will be dealt with later. Meanwhile, it must be acknowledged that all the virulent and corrosive qualities implicit in the words etching, needle, biting, all the quality of blackness implicit in the word ink, combined to serve a passionate temperament obsessed with man and woman's cruellest and darkest powers.

In England, where admiration for the Dutch masters had never flagged, the too little known etchings of Constable and Old Crome contributed much to the discovery of the world of nature. The influence of these two can be traced in Girtin's work as well as in Turner's *Liber Studiorum*. By the latter, Turner freed landscape painting from existing conventions, whereas the over-praised work of David Wilkie and Andrew Geddes suffers from being still too derivative.

In Germany, Chodowiecki's witty vignettes, and the work of J.-C. Reinhardt, Dora, Koch and the Quaglios (German by origin but established in Rome) belong by imagination and execution to the 18th century. In the work of

JOHN CROME, called OLD CROME. *Tree.* Etching

JOSEPH MALLORD WILLIAM TURNER. *Ben Arthur, Scotland. 1807-19.*
Plate from 'Liber Studiorum'. Dry point and aquatint

Kobbe, Dillis, Gabler, Erhard, Klein, Kobell, and that of Kyhn in Denmark,
on the other hand, a wholly new concept of light can be seen to be emerging.

One reason why direct etching was so little practised in France at the beginning
of the 19th century is that the classical line engraving was still in favour officially.
But besides this, painters were also attracted by the entirely new process of
lithography. In Spain, Goya the unique had no successors. In France, the
only known etching by Géricault is his *The Dapple-Grey* (c. 1817) and the only
one by Ingres his portrait of the Archbishop *Courtois de Pressigny,* executed in
Rome in 1816. The latter is outstanding for its clarity and simplicity and compa-
rable, for intensity of expression, authority of gesture and economy of line, as
well as for the silvery tone that is only obtained by slow biting, with the best
of Van Dyck's portrait engravings.

Delacroix's contribution to etching was more important. The earliest plates
we possess are very free copies done after Rembrandt's *Abraham and Isaac* and
Resurrection, while his aquatints *Interior Scene* and *Hospital Interior* plainly owe

JEAN-AUGUSTE DOMINIQUE INGRES. *Gabriel Courtois de Pressigny.* *1816.* Etching

AMBROSIUS GABLER. *The Edge of the Wood.* Etching

much to Goya. But for the real Delacroix we must look forward to his *Turk Mounting a Horse* which is worthy to hang beside the best of English or French aquatints, his *Royal Tiger* and, above all, to the six plates executed in 1833 but published only in 1865. *The Jewess of Algiers,* drawn after his return from Morocco, is a masterpiece of concision. With admirable clarity, his needle has traced the body and draperies, brought the background to life and made light scintillate between the lines, while the richness of the parts left white rivals that of the blacks. The aquatints entitled *The Blacksmith, Arabs in Oran* and *Reclining woman seen from behind* (Delacroix's only etching of a nude, which has all the economy of line of a Rembrandt) have a tone as rich as the most glowing water-colours.

Only one etching by Delacroix's friend Bonington is known, the *View of Bologna,* and likewise only one by Barye, *Stag and Lynx* (1834). A large number exists of works by another of Delacroix's friends, Paul Huet. His great stormy landscapes, with their too heavily laden and deeply bitten skies, recall at once

DOMENICO QUAGLIO. *Courtyard in Munich. c. 1815.* Etching

RICHARD PARKES BONINGTON. *View of Bologna.* *c. 1826.* Etching

EUGÈNE DELACROIX. *The Jewess of Algiers. 1833.* Etching

GABRIEL-ALEXANDRE DECAMPS. *Turkish Bodyguards. 1834.* Lithograph

those of the English landscape engravers, Wilkie and Geddes, and their predecessors the Dutch masters, besides also looking forward to the work of Théodore
Rousseau, in particular his *Portfolio of Six Etchings* published in 1835.

Following on and akin to Delacroix's series of etchings, come Chassériau's
fifteen plates illustrating *Othello* (1844), with their clean lines incised and bitten
by the artist himself. More static in their Romanticism, they yet plainly owe
much to Delacroix but, whereas the latter used lithography for his illustrations
of Gœthe, Walter Scott and Shakespeare, Chassériau chose etching for his
Othello as also for his very rare *Death of Cleopatra.* 'In the plate showing the
Moor killing his love, as in the later one showing his despair beside Desdemona's couch', wrote Roger-Marx, 'Chassériau reached heights of tragedy that
Delacroix himself never surpassed. When depicting love and grief, he becomes
greater than himself. Throughout all the drama's vicissitudes, he preserves
for Desdemona the sculptural attitudes that the rhythm of the line demands.
In all his drawings of women, Chassériau succeeds in making the very idea of
an abrupt movement or gesture appear an insult to their beauty.'

Decamps was a skilful and prolific showman and his *March-past of Cimbrians*

THÉODORE CHASSÉRIAU. *Othello: The Death of Desdemona. 1844.* Etching

and Teutons, Turkish Bodyguards and *Old Beggar-woman,* show both virtuosity and a certain truculence. His imagination, however, is not always equal to his powers of execution.

After the success achieved in England by steel engravings such as those of Turner for illustrating keepsakes and travel books, many of the French Romantic school were commissioned to ornament texts with lively vignettes. Eugène Lami, as well as Alfred and Tony Johannot, excelled at this kind of fine work, producing frontispieces, tailpieces and ornamented letters in which the spirit of the century of Fragonard was allied to that of contemporary Gothic. Few frontispieces are better than those of Célestin Nanteuil, whose qualities of vision allied to a craftsman's technical skill enabled him to achieve greatness within a small compass. In the page-headings he designed for his novelist and poet friends, a sense of wonder is skilfully allied with an instinctive understanding of the potentialities of the copper as a medium. There has never been a better embodiment of the Romantic spirit and its dreams than Nanteuil, and his inspired vignettes look forward to the work of Rodolphe Bresdin.

The 'small etching' provided a technique perfectly adapted to Meissonier's powers, as also to those of Charles Jacques who, though often betrayed by his own facility, yet had a real gift for calculating the times needed for biting in plates. Hervier, a fop but an attractive fop, can also be counted a Romantic. The agreeable and picturesque quality of his work, which, especially in his seascapes, recalls that of Isabey, was combined with a vitality all his own.

WOOD ENGRAVING IN ILLUSTRATION

Except for purposes of illustration, original wood cuts or engravings had been as much neglected by painters as etching. But after the success of the publication in London in 1828 of the *Fables* with Harvey's illustrations, the caricaturists and other of their contemporaries found a ready market for ink drawings done on small wood blocks. The use of wood blocks cut along the grain now gave way to that of cross-grain blocks. The graver was used by skilful interpreters to reproduce in facsimile the designs of Charlet, Daumier, Gavarni, Grandville, Jean Gigoux, Henri Monnier, Raffet, Tony Johannot, Decamps, Daubigny, Meissonier, Vernet, Célestin Nanteuil, Dauzats or Eugène Lami.

The *Magasin pittoresque* established in 1833, the *Musée des Familles,* and publishers such as Curmer, Furne, Gosselin and Hetzel followed the example set by the English publisher Thomson in commissioning many vignettes, the charm of which was scarcely diminished when interpreted by Brévière, Porret, Godart fils, Lavieille, Birouste and the trio Andrew, Best and Leloir.

Meissonier, nicknamed by Degas king of the dwarfs, Jean Gigoux and Tony Johannot excelled at this small-scale work, but it is our great misfortune that Daumier should almost always have had to work within such narrow limits.

THOMAS SHOTTER BOYS. *The Pavillon de Flore. 1839.* Hand coloured lithograph

ERNEST MEISSONIER. *Fishermen.* Etching

Honoré Daumier. *Medical Nemesis. 1840.* Wood engraving

Nevertheless, even in pocket-sized works such as his seven *Character Studies* (the *Poet,* the *Concierge,* etc.), or the *Portfolios of Sketches,* he still succeeds in giving the slightest sketch the style of an epic. From 1833 onwards, he produced more than a thousand wood engravings for *La Caricature, Le Charivari, Le Monde Illustré* and the *Journal pour tous,* as well as for the *Français peints par eux-mêmes,* the *Musée parisien,* the *Mystères de Paris* and the *Comédie Humaine.* The illustrations, on a larger scale than the vignettes, which decorate the *Medical Nemesis* (1840) and the series entitled *Licensed Valuers* make one regret that it never occurred to a publisher to commission Daumier, rather than Doré, to illustrate a text such as Don Quixote that would have been worthy of his skill.

But it would be unfair to belittle an epoch during which wood engraving still remembered its origins and in which the bad colouring and heavy detail beloved of Pisan and his followers were still unknown. These, in their attempts to rival the etchers, loaded the wood engraving with additions in which its original qualities of strength and clear-cut line were lost.

The charming lithographs done by Tony Johannot and Célestin Nanteuil (the latter with his three thousand vignettes produced in twenty years for one hundred and fifty different books) can almost be considered original work, their interpreters having done no more than copy the pen designs exactly. Both

HONORÉ DAUMIER. *Medical Nemesis. 1840.* Wood engraving

these artists were too fully occupied in illustration work to have time to make any independent plates. Illustrations such as those for *Gil Blas* by Jean Gigoux, for *Lazarillo de Torrès, Paul et Virginie* and the *Contes rémois* by Meissonier, for *Portes de fer* by Dauzats, for the *Diable à Paris* on which Devéria, Charlet, Grandville, Paul Huet and Daubigny all collaborated, or for the *Histoire de Napoléon* by Raffet are typical of the taste of the time. They were followed a little later by the eighty-five small wood engravings designed by Gustave Doré as illustrations for the *Contes drolatiques,* in which the artist has succeeded in expressing more gaiety and often more grandeur than are to be found in many larger works.

In Germany, Gubitz, followed by Blasius Höfel in Vienna, had brought wood engravings back into fashion. The symbolism of Caspar David Fried-

HONORÉ DAUMIER. *In the Café. c. 1840.* Wood

rich's work is inspired by a genuine love of nature and foreshadows the work of the Pre-Raphaelites. From 1840 onwards, wood engraving as a method of illustration enjoyed a new vogue under the influence of what was known as the Nazarene school. Menzel's powers of observation and vivid imagination reached their culmination in his illustrations for the *Œuvres de Frédéric le Grand* which can be regarded as a pendant to Raffet's *Napoléon*. Among the artists who contributed towards the revival of original wood engraving were W. Friedrich and Savino. It came closest to its primitive form in the works of Moritz von Schwind who drew heavily on German folklore, Ludwig Richter and, still more, the Romantic Rethel, though the last-named fell perhaps too much under the influence of Dürer and Holbein, especially in his *Dance of Death*.

CASPAR DAVID FRIEDRICH. *Woman on a Mountain.* Woodcut

ALFRED RETHEL. *The Dance of Death.* c. 1845. Wood engraving

WILLIAM BLAKE. *The River of Life*. Lithograph

In England, William Blake (1757-1827) was a visionary who stands alone. He expressed his visions partly on stone and partly on wood. Much of his inspiration comes from the dramatists and Michelangelo.

After 1841, English wood engraving, which was already serving as a model for French artists, increased rapidly in popularity as a result of the work of Samuel Williams, designer and engraver of the illustrations for Thomson's *The Seasons*, of John Gilbert's illustrations to Shakespeare and Forster's pastoral scenes.

So far as comic illustrations were concerned, Cruikshank, who was a copious contributor to the *Comic Almanack*, used wood in preference to copper, and

WILHELM BUSCH. *Comic.* Woodcut

so did John Leech and Charles Keene, the kindlier and less extravagant successors of Gillray and Rowlandson. In Constantin Guys, whose drawings in pen and ink wash were immediately reproduced as wood engravings, *The Illustrated London News* found a highly original, at times Rembrandtesque, reporter.

English comic illustrators had their imitators in Germany where the *Fliegende Blätter* was founded in 1844. For this publication, Pocci (largely influenced by Töpffer), Spitzweg and, above all, Wilhelm Busch (1832-1908) produced a variety of straightforward humorous drawings of a vigorous and homely kind, although at the same time not without their poetic side, even if they never attained the tragi-comic vision and the style of Daumier's work.

WILHELM BUSCH. *Comic.* Woodcut

ORIGINS AND DEVELOPMENT OF LITHOGRAPHY

THE FIRST LITHOGRAPHERS

The process of lithography was discovered in 1796, in Bavaria, by Aloysius Senefelder, as the result of one of those lucky chances which, in art as in medicine, have often been the origin of great inventions. When Senefelder, whose dream was to become a dramatic author and write comedies like those of Molière, discovered lithography (or, as it was first called in England, polyautography), he certainly never imagined how quickly the process would be accepted and how many new techniques it would suggest; still less that, within half a century, it would successfully challenge both wood and copperplate engraving.

The discovery of lithography resulted from the accidental transfer of the writing on a washing bill to the stone on which it had been left lying, and Senefelder's first idea was only that the process might be used by printers for reproducing prospectuses, musical scores, and other similar texts. Even in Germany itself,

CARLE VERNET. *English Travellers.* *c. 1820.* Lithograph

the use made by a few amateurs of the stone blocks of fine Munich granite was only the pulling of a small number of impressions. It had not yet been realised that here was a totally new process.

What strikes us most in the earliest lithographs is largely the pleasure their authors obviously experienced at discovering the similarity between the grain of the stone and the stippling carried out by engravers. Most of them are greyish in tone and testify to the hesitant way in which the greasy crayon has been applied to the surface of the stone. Regarded as first attempts, they are not without merit, but those experimenting in this hitherto unknown field were, for the most part, second-rate artists and it was not until later that any real vitality was infused into the process by serious innovators as opposed to dilettantes.

There is no need, therefore, to linger over the first clumsy attempts made in Munich by Mettenleiter, Mayrhoffer, Winter, Wagenbauer and Hauber and, subsequently, in Düsseldorf and in Austria. Among a flood of weak and characterless likenesses, one or two portraits by Krüger, Friedrich Jentzen, Gustav Feckert, Lieder and Kriehuber stand out, and lithography was also used by Strixner and Pelotti to produce a more or less faithful series of reproductions after Dürer or the earlier masters.

In England, the Swiss-born Fuseli attempted, like Blake, to illustrate the works of Milton but, as was later the case with Redon, he lacked the qualities needed to grasp the poet's inner meaning.

Towards 1815, in France, two printers, the Comte de Lasteyrie and Engelmann, popularised the new process, news of which had already been published in Paris in 1802 by one of Senefelder's collaborators. Lithographs produced included the *Portrait of the Painter Susemihl* by Boilly, the *Flying Mercury* by Bergeret,

JEAN-ANTOINE GROS. *Desert Arab. 1817.* Lithograph

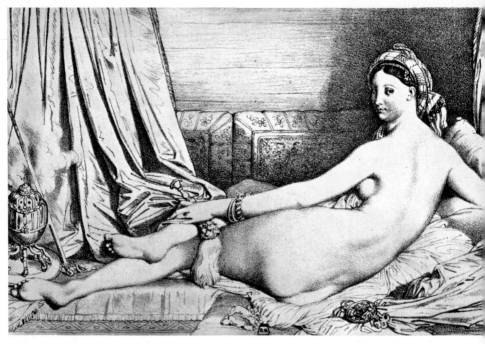

JEAN-AUGUSTE DOMINIQUE INGRES. *Reclining Odalisque. 1825.* Lithograph

Baron Lejeune's *Cossack*, the *Portrait of Staininger* by Colonel Lomet, the *Holy Family* by Vivant-Denon, a few male figures by Girodet-Trioson, two allegorical figures, *The Idler* and *The Watcher,* by Guérin, some country scenes by Desmarais and topographical engravings by Bacler D'Albe, a few scenes taken from mythology by Hersent, Marlet's Paris street scenes and the *scènes galantes* of Evariste Fragonard. Carle Vernet, renowned for his studies of horses, had a far larger output. So, too, did his son Horace who, like Swebach, specialised in military and equestrian pictures.

But none of these were much more than rather timid experiments. Their laborious execution makes them look like tracings, and they are deficient in the power of direct attack to be found a few years later in the work of various artists of the first rank who, at the suggestion of Lasteyrie or Engelmann, began to draw directly on the stone, in preference to preparing designs for subsequent transfer.

There are two plates by Gros that just deserve mention. Although their execution is elementary and they are of a uniform grey tone, one of them, the *Desert Arab,* engraved in 1817, anticipates to some extent the work of Géricault by the strength and firmness of its drawing.   Another similar, although later work, the *Odalisque* of Ingres, published in one of Delpech's portfolios, is somewhat too obviously done after a painting and, in spite of its flowing lines, lacks the force and vigour of the artist's paintings and drawings of nudes.

As for Rude's *Neopolitan Fisherman,* printed by Motte in about 1833, its uniform grain is so reminiscent of Alophe's work that it is hardly surprising that Béraldi queried the attribution to Rude.

It is greatly to be regretted that Prud'hon did so little original engraving and left his work to be interpreted by Copia and Roger.   His *Reading Aloud* and *An Unfortunate Family* show what his gift for exquisite modelling and delicate drawing, resembling that of Fantin-Latour, could have produced had he adopted the new method.

Francesco de Goya. *Spanish Diversion. 1825.* Lithograph

41

NICOLAS-TOUSSAINT CHARLET. *French Dragoon with Flag.* *1818.* Lithograph

NICOLAS-TOUSSAINT CHARLET. *The Baptism of Fire. c. 1818.* Lithograph

It was only occasionally, then, that the best painters overcame their suspicion of grained stone as a medium sufficiently to allow them to make use of it. Of the active group assembled by Lasteyrie, which included the two Vernets, Eugène Lami, Devéria, Girodet, Marlet, Demarne, Michallon, Henriquel-Dupont, the Belgian artist Odevaere, and Charlet, it was only the latter, so unjustifiably neglected today, who, as water-colourist and painter, really grasped the possibilities of lithography and recognised it for what it was, a new language. By varying the number of crayons used, he succeeded in producing an infinite variety of gradations in his blacks and was constantly enriching his work with the results of fresh discoveries made during the course of its execution.

In lithography, the even pressure of the etching needle is replaced by the use of pen or crayon and of ink diluted to the extent necessary to ensure the degree

43

THÉODORE GÉRICAULT. *The Retreat from Moscow.* *c. 1812.* Lithograph

of transparency desired. A dark, velvety tone is thus produced, highlights being introduced by the skilful use of the scraper. With the appearance in 1819 of lithographic aquatint, it became possible to embellish the prints by the addition of various types of colouring. Within a few years, however, lithography was showing itself capable of interpreting the most varied range of effects and sentiments, and able to display such qualities of warmth and sensibility, so perfectly attuned to the Romantic ideal, that it was in due course adopted by Géricault, Goya, Delacroix, Bonington, Barye, Daumier, Raffet, Devéria, Gavarni and Decamps alike, and even for a time displaced etching as a method of engraving.

ORIGINAL LITHOGRAPHERS: GOYA, CHARLET, GÉRICAULT, DELACROIX

The greatest praise is due to Charlet for having been the first to instill some true vitality into lithography. Although his execution was not outstanding, he possessed a degree of creative energy that should not be underestimated. He had something of the lyric quality of a Gros, and Delacroix, who never faltered in admiration for his work, singled out for special praise the fact that, prolific as he was, never once did he repeat a head or a movement or, whether he was portraying soldiers, working men or Paris urchins, fail to give each his own distinguishing mark. Delacroix said he had the secret of expressing the sublime in terms of the natural. When he put Charlet beside Molière or La Fontaine as a portrayer of character, Delacroix may have exaggerated; that is a place to which only Daumier can aspire. But it is nevertheless true that Charlet, the son of a dragoon from Sambre-et-Meuse, when re-living his own heroic years, with all their tears and their trivialities, scaled without difficulty the summits of emotion. His old soldier and his young recruit facing his baptism of fire are equally immortal figures. Whether he is portraying a flag-bearer, a rifleman or a cavalryman, they are all real, alive, individual. His engravings, though large, are filled with detail and foreshadow almost all that is best in Géricault's work, and are infinitely superior to anything done by either of the two Vernets or Bellanger.

The popularity enjoyed by Charlet's work under the French Restoration undoubtedly contributed to the vogue for lithography which found an early outlet in the form of illustrations for books such as Baron Taylor's *Voyages pittoresques et romantiques dans l'ancienne France*. The process was adopted simultaneously in all countries, by good and bad artists alike, all stimulated by young printers trained in Engelmann's methods.

One of the latter was Gaulon of Bordeaux, known to us by Goya's portrait of him. By 1819, the author of the *Caprices* had already carried out one or two experiments on stone in Madrid, which included the *Old Woman spinning*, the *Duel in the Spanish Tradition, The Monk,* the *Amorous Couple, The Force of Love, Woman*

EDOUARD MANET. *Punchinello*. *1874*. Colour lithograph using seven stones

reading aloud and *Sleep*. While in exile he reverted to the method once more and, after one or two plates such as *El vito: an Andalusian Dance* and the two portraits of *M. Gaulon* and *M. Gaulon's son,* executed in 1825, produced the series of much larger lithographs of bullfighting which may be described as the first masterpieces to be produced on stone. Goya's habit was to cover his stone with a greyish ground and then prop it up on an easel as though it were a canvas. He would stand in front of it, moving to and fro to judge his effects, intensifying a line here or a shadow there with his always blunt crayon, using the scraper to bring out highlights. In short, he worked like a painter and his dynamic force, coupled with an inspiration even greater than that which produced the *Tauromaquia* aquatints, resulted in the four great compositions: *The Famous American Mariano Ceballos, Bravo Toro, Spanish Diversion* and *The Divided Arena,* to which can perhaps be added a fifth that has only recently been discovered. Although his sight had by that time become so impaired by age that he is said to have had to use a magnifying glass, none of Goya's other work shows more youth or spontaneity. Delacroix, whose admiration for the *Caprices* was unbounded, is said to have managed to procure a set of the bullfighting lithographs. It is a symphony in black and white in which light and movement are merged in one, in which each detail surprised from life is yet subordinated to the design of the whole, and in which the accessory touches (an animal charging or kicking, a gored picador, the excitement of the aficionados in the audience) are introduced with short, sensitive, masterly strokes.

In relation to the first masterpieces produced by the French lithographers, the bullfight lithographs come seven years after Géricault's *Horses fighting in a Stable, The Boxers* and *The Hospital Waggon* with which Goya was in all probability unacquainted, and belong to the same year as Delacroix's first engraved masterpiece, *Macbeth consulting the Witches,* which succeeded one or two youthful experiments and which in almost every line proclaims the debt owed to Goya.

A similar dynamic force distinguishes the work of Goya, Géricault and Delacroix and they were the first, after Gros and Charlet, to translate it into terms of crayon and stone. The development reserved for lithography was to prove such that it is safe to say that, had Rembrandt returned to earth then, it would have been lithography that he adopted as his technique.

The engravings produced by Géricault between 1817 and 1823 amount, in addition to a single experiment in etching, to some hundred plates. Of these, seventy-five were executed by himself, the rest having suffered somewhat from his collaboration with Volmar, Léon Cogniet, Charlet or Eugène Lami. Géricault may owe to Carle Vernet, his first master, his passion for making studies of thoroughbreds, but his temperament makes him far closer to Charlet. He was to end by surpassing Charlet, but he learnt a great deal from him on the technical side.

Roman Butchers, his first attempt at a lithograph, and his *Standard-bearer* which, in treatment, resembles an etching and looks back to the work of the Dutch masters, show him still feeling his way. But, beginning the following year, his *Mameluke defending a Wounded Trumpeter, Artillery Manœuvre, The Hospital*

THÉODORE GÉRICAULT. *Entrance to the Adelphi Wharf. 1821.* Lithograph

Waggon, Horses fighting in a Stable and *Swiss Guard at the Louvre,* produced when he was still under thirty, entitled him to be regarded—as Burty wrote of him in 1861—as the father of the modern school both of engraving and painting, as much for his freedom of execution as for his power of conveying movement, his sensitive composition and the charm of his forms.

Drawn with pen or greasy crayon, these pages of Napoleonic history through which, as Delacroix says in his *Journal,* there seems to breathe something of the genius of Michelangelo, show Géricault to be a master of chiaroscuro. If the term Romantic artist means one in whom temperament reaches the sublime but passion never becomes uncontrolled, then Géricault was a Romantic. He evokes history in a way that brings him nearer to Gros than to David, though

48

THÉODORE GÉRICAULT. *Pity the sorrows of a poor old man.* *1821.* Lithograph

it can be said of him even more truly than of Gros that, fellow-countryman as he was of Corneille and Poussin, he possessed that special nervous force and gift of audacity which are to painting what the comic sense is to the theatre; whoever possesses them has licence to disobey the rules. He was the forerunner not only of Delacroix who wrote these words, but of Raffet, Daumier, Barye, Carpeaux, Guys and Rodin.

In *Retreat from Moscow* Géricault made use for the first time of a new procedure invented by himself, which consisted in employing a second, or 'tint', stone. Elsewhere in his work the sense of style evident in each composition, the skilful reproduction of even the most insignificant movements, the effects of light and shade, are achieved by the use of ink or crayon only. During his stay in London

THÉODORE GÉRICAULT. *The Boxers. 1818.* Lithograph

with Charlet (1821) he did a series of six plates with a pen, on a kind of cardboard
known as 'stone paper' which had a rough, irregular surface. The series was
entitled *The Jockey* and was somewhat severe in execution. But he soon abandoned this substitute material in favour of good Munich stone, which he used
for the most beautiful series of plates he ever produced. These were printed
by Hullmandel, and are full of vigour. They consist of twelve powerful drawings
intitled *Various Subjects*, three-quarters of which are equestrian studies (*Horse
going to a Fair, A Party of Life Guards, Horses excercising, The Coal Wagon, The
Flemish, English* and *French Farrier,* etc.), while the remainder are every-day
street scenes and contain some of his best work (*The Piper, The Poor Old Man,
Entrance to the Adelphi Wharf* and the *Paralysed Woman*).

On his return to Paris, he did a further series of twelve *Studies of Horses* and followed them by a portfolio on four different subjects. These works, together with a series in which he collaborated with Volmar and Léon Cogniet somewhat to the detriment of his usual lightness of touch, and some illustrations for *The Bride of Abydos, The Giaour* and *Mazeppa*, are far from showing the same simple sense of the tragic, the candour and the inspiration of the great series of English plates in which, in his own phrase, he had abandoned Parnassus for the stables.

'Michelangelo, the masks of antiquity and Géricault', wrote Delacroix acknowledging his debt to the artist, 'who is opening up such infinite horizons and authorizing any and every innovation.' It is impossible not to recognise the affinity that exists between Delacroix's *Combat of the Giaour and the Pasha* (1827) and the *Mameluke defending a Wounded Trumpeter* (1818), or between the *Horse brought down by a Tiger* (1828) and the *Horse devoured by a Lion* (1823), even Delacroix's titles seeming to be derived from Géricault.

Delacroix, as we have seen, began by using copper, the first plates he made being some very free interpretations of Rembrandt. He was still under thirty

THÉODORE GÉRICAULT. *Horses fighting in a Stable. 1818.* Lithograph

EUGÈNE DELACROIX. *Macbeth consulting the Witches.* *1825.* Lithograph

when he copied *Abraham and Isaac* and *The Resurrection of Lazarus* (c. 1816). Several years later he produced three plates inspired by the Greek wars and representing Turks or Mamelukes mounting, saddling or reining-in their horses. Everything combined to influence him in favour of lithography and of following the example of his friends Géricault, Fielding and Bonington. Both his *Journal* and his *Letters* show where his tastes lay: 'Bought an early lithography by Géricault in the rue des Saints-Pères ... Went round to Gihaut to select some Géricaults ... Got some splendid ideas ... Charges in the manner of Goya.'

His *Macbeth consulting the Witches* (1825) is of capital importance, not only in his own work, but in the history of lithography. This has never been sufficiently recognised. Not published until 1864 in the *Artiste*, the whole picture has been gone over with the scraper or, it would be more accurate to say, was conceived like a mezzotint, following the method introduced by Tudot which Charlet was one of the first to adopt and which was afterwards followed by Eugène Isabey, Devéria and many others.

In a letter dated 1843, Delacroix describes his technique to one of his pupils: 'Once you have drawn your picture in charcoal on the stone, rub until you have shaped it as you want. Then take a scraper and remove as much of the black as you think necessary, but taking care not to uncover the grain of the stone. Don't be too timid; you will soon find out the trick for yourself.'

Delacroix, after publishing in 1825 a series entitled *Studies after Classical Coins,* an example of the analysis of form '*par noyaux*', continued to combine the use of ink and scraper to produce the following works: the *Combat of the Giaour and the Pasha,* a set of illustrations for *Faust,* published by Motte in 1828, a set of illustrations for *Hamlet* (1834-43), the *Horse brought down by a Tiger* (1828), the *Lion from the Atlas Mountains,* the *Royal Tiger,* the *Tiger Cub playing with its Mother,* the *Frightened Horse leaving the Water,* and the *Wild Horse brought down by a Tiger* amongst others. He used both aquatint and the pen to produce additional variety in his plates. Like etchings, lithographs do not allow of many states. 'In lithography,' wrote Delacroix, 'retouching is almost impossible and in any case always destroys something of the design's original freshness.' In the margin of some of the proofs of the *Faust* and *Hamlet* illustrations can be seen a series of little sketches — horses, wild animals, nudes — done from memory or suggested by the shape of marks on the paper, in which Delacroix was trying out his pen or crayon, or testing the quality of wash. In the case of other works such as the *Muleteers in Tétuan, Women of Algiers, Women hanging out Washing in Tangiers,* done after his return from Morocco, or in *Hercules and Antaeus,* he has 'autographed' them with his pen only.

An indefatigable worker, but discouraged by the total lack of success of his engravings and busy by that time with large decorative pieces, Delacroix was only to produce three more plates to complete his Shakespearean series (*The Death of Ophelia, Hamlet and Horatio with the Gravediggers* and *Hamlet and Laertes*), and seven plates for *Goetz von Berlichingen* (1836-43). He had no more time to waste on what, with a touch of contempt, he described as little things.

But what he called little things we today can call great. It cannot be denied

EUGÈNE DELACROIX. *Royal Tiger. 1829.* Lithograph

that taste has altered since the days of unbridled Romanticism which produced his *Faust* illustrations, some of them done in 1827 after he had seen the play in London and far too reminiscent of the theatre and the exaggerated style of the English actors, or his more melodramatic compositions inspired by Shakespeare, Otway, Tasso, Sir Walter Scott or Byron ('Look up some of Byron's lines to whip up your imagination,' he wrote in his *Journal*).   Today we prefer the engravings in which he is not concerned with illustration or with bringing history to life, but simply following his own inspiration and expressing what he liked to call his 'private' life.   *Macbeth consulting the Witches* is one of his earlier lithographs and ante-dates his *Faust*, but it is superior to most of his other Shakespearean pieces because of the simplicity of his presentation of the marvellous. For the same reason, we may well regret that he did not follow the example set by himself in his brilliant etchings of every-day scenes (the *Blacksmith* or the *Reclining woman seen from behind*) and produce more lithographs based on immediate reactions; scenes observed, for instance, during his walks with Barye in the Jardin des Plantes.

It is a pity that Barye himself should have produced so few engravings. All we have, in addition to his single etching, are some ten small lithographs, many of which *(A Lioness and her Cubs, Sleeping Tiger, Study of a Cat* and especially *the Mississippi Bear)* are extraordinarily vigorous. They are real portraits, and, in their strict accuracy, as generally representative of their species as though they were the work of a Buffon. Their technique is simple and there is no 'cheating'. Using only a tapered crayon, Barye distinguishes between the different substances he is depicting almost without the need to rub out or use the scraper. With what sureness of touch and infinite ease he traces the forms and suggests the background, and the idea of movement even in repose, even in the case of captive animals that could only be observed from behind bars.

ANTOINE-LOUIS BARYE. *Mississippi Bear. c. 1835.* Lithograph

RICHARD PARKES BONINGTON. *The Clock-Tower.* *1824.* Lithograph

NEWTON FIELDING. *The Stag.* *1828.* Lithograph

At the same period, another portrayer of animals, also a friend of Delacroix, was producing lithographs in much greater quantity. Newton Fielding, who also produced charming water colours, was unlike Barye in using every resource offered by lithography and aquatint for studies of tame, as well as wild, animals and birds. If Barye can be compared to Daumier for the height and stance of his models, Fielding can be compared to Devéria for his tender blending of densest blacks into quietest greys, as well as for what might be called his familiar treatment of the most dangerous species.

Parkes Bonington's early death in 1824 prevented him from following up his vibrant and tempestuous landscapes which certainly owed something to the influence of Turner. He produced a series of delicate and distinguished lithographs which were published partly in the numbers of the *Voyages pittoresques et romantiques dans l'ancienne France* dealing with Normandy and Franche-Comté (*Clock-Tower at Rouen, Rouen Cathedral, View of Evreux*), and partly in the *Restes*

Célestin-François Nanteuil-Lebœuf. *The Drummer's Bride.* *1835*. Lithograph

et fragments d'architecture du Moyen Age. The name of Bonington cannot be mentioned without recalling that of Boys, who matched him in delicacy and sensibility. Boys was one of the precursors of coloured lithography, as can be seen from his views of Paris such as the *Pavillon de Flore,* and his topographical prints.

Almost a century has been needed to assign their true place to the occasional engravers whose work was apt to be placed by contemporary amateurs and publishers considerably below the prolific output of the professional and specialised engravers. These were taking advantage of the growing vogue for lithographs to show infinite ingenuity and powers of adaptation in producing the innumerable varieties of publication demanded by the fashion of the time: albums designed for adults as well as for children, illustrated books, rebuses, portraits, landscapes, or genre pieces, all of which were being published between 1825 and 1860 by Motte, Delpech, Gihaut, Lemercier, Ritter, Martinet, Delaunois, Villain, Bry, Wild, Frey, Bertaut, etc.

Here it must suffice to mention the attractive work produced by the Parisian Henri Monnier, the fashionable chronicler, and that of Eugène Lami, who also started out in London by making pen drawings for lithographs and produced a number of prints showing fêtes, balls, hunts, races and military occasions. Another artist worthy of mention is Pigal, who made frequent use of colour in his engravings. He was one of the first to take an interest in scenes of popular life and, although he did not possess Daumier's lively fancy, he nevertheless sympathised with the lower-middle and working classes, and was quite capable, if necessary, of pointing a moral *(Rake's Progress)*.

LOUIS-ADOLPHE HERVIER. *Cul-de-Sac in Trouville. 1848.* Lithograph

EUGÈNE ISABEY. *The Return to Harbour.* *1839.* Lithograph

LANDSCAPE LITHOGRAPHY

A true innovator in the field of landscape lithography is to be found in Jean-
Baptiste Isabey (1803-1886), the son of the miniaturist, whose original ambition
was to be a sailor, and who subsequently devoted his best talents to depicting
harbour scenes and estuaries. In his engravings the world of sky and water
seems an integral part of the life of man. Isabey was one of the illustrators of
Baron Taylor's *Voyages* (L'Auvergne), and his first seascapes appeared in a
portfolio to which a number of artists contributed, including Charlet, Gavarni,
Roqueplan, Lepoitevin, Mozin, Brascassat, Lemercier, Gigoux and Lami. In
these works, as well as in his first mezzotint, *Low Tide,* and the series of six
engravings entitled *Souvenirs (Caen, Rouen, Saint-Valéry, Dieppe, Bretagne, Finistère),*
he expresses himself far more freely than in the later series of lithographs after
his own paintings, in which the treatment is less sympathetic and where there
is often a superfluity of detail. The attraction of his work lies in his power of

61

conveying the poetry to be found in river or seascape. His very ink seems to exhale the mingled odours of tar and spray, and the warmth of his shadows is heightened by the vigour of his strokes. With his skill in observing the atmospheric variations that govern each of his scenes, with his receptivity and decisiveness, allied to his care for precise detail, as exemplified in such works as the *The Return to Harbour*, Isabey provides a foretaste of the genius of the greatest of his pupils, Jongkind.

Hervier (1818-1879) resembles Isabey in many ways. A devoted explorer of the French provinces, he brought a similar lively mind to the perception and delineation of the picturesque medieval remains to be found in their old cities, and the bustling activity of their markets and ports. Some of his smaller plates recall those of Bresdin. By using a magnifying glass one can obtain the illusion of getting right inside them and they almost merit the adjective great. Hervier found an unsuspected poetry in detail which he reproduced with loving skill. His lithographs *(Landscapes, Seascapes, Hovels,* 1843) interpret as faithfully as his etchings the childlike joy he found in exercising his powers of observation.

PAUL HUET. *View of Avignon. 1834.* Etching

CAMILLE PISSARRO. *Church and Farm at Eragny. 1890.* Coloured etching

Paul Huet's seascapes are contemporary with those of Isabey and treated in much the same manner. There is a strong personal element in his series of small lithographed landscapes done in 1829, and in his delicate views of Versailles and Saint-Cloud. In his feeling for the mystery of trees he forestalled the Barbizon school, as can be seen in his etchings and mezzotints which, though somewhat overburdened with detail, are nevertheless full of light (*The Heron, The Two Cottages, The Flood*), while their romanticism recalls the landscapes of Old Crome and, through him, the work of Rembrandt.

The few lithographs produced by Dupré date from his youth between 1835 and 1839, and came out in *Artiste (Grazing in the Limousin, Windmill at Sologne, The Banks of the Somme, English Scene)*. They are full of light and space and foreshadow the future masterpieces of Corot, Daubigny and Théodore Rousseau.

These are men who stand out head and shoulders above a host of minor artists who, in Germany and England, regarded lithography and wood engraving as merely a means of livelihood and had no ambition beyond being illustrators. Many of them, in spite of having little turn for satire, gladly enrolled themselves under Philippon's banner, regarding lithography as a quick and useful weapon for the daily castigation of those in power.

This brings us to consideration of that great revolutionary movement which was to bring sudden popularity to a process still in its infancy, and provide it with an impetus that no one could have foreseen.

DAUMIER AND THE STAFF OF 'LA CARICATURE'
GAVARNI, DEVÉRIA, DECAMPS, RAFFET, CHASSÉRIAU

La Caricature, bearing the motto *Castigat ridendo mores,* first appeared on 4th November 1830, and continued for two hundred and fifty-one issues, the last of which came out on 27th August 1835. From the hundredth number onwards, *La Caricature* added the adjective 'political' to its former description of itself as a 'moral, religious and theatrical' publication. Charles Philippon, the editor, seems at first to have been uncertain exactly what slant to give his weekly. He began by employing a whole series of artists, capable of using lithography to treat the most varied subjects without distinguishing to any great extent between them. His contributors at that time included Charlet, Devéria, Pigal, Paul Huet, Decamps, Raffet, Traviès, Adam, Wattier, Lepoitevin, Jules David, Jeanson, Numa, Grandville and Henri Monnier.

One of the keenest of these was Monnier, the pupil of Gros. At once a painter, an actor and a writer, Monnier was among the earliest to make pen drawings on stone which were subsequently enhanced by the addition of colour. The influence of English drawing and caricature, and especially of Cruikshank's work, is plainly to be seen in Monnier's early series (1823) of lithographs, several of which were published in London. Monnier specialized in scenes of every-day life and street types *(Quizzes à la Mode, Parisian Sketches, Bureaucracy, Contrasts, Grisettes).* There is no malice in the short legends attached to each of his sketches. Like most of his own figures, Monnier was a detached observer, and his charm consists in the cheerfulness and good nature of his humour, although he often stepped out of character to become a political satirist in creating types such as *Monsieur Prudhomme.*

Another caricaturist to achieve fame by inventing a type was Traviès, although subsequent improvements made to his somewhat uninspired original sketch owed much to the influence of Daumier. For the cover sheet of *La Caricature* Philippon commissioned Grandville (1803-1847). His *Today's Metamorphoses* and *Scenes from Animal Public Life* (1842) indicate a poetic imagination and a sense of the bizarre bordering on fantasy, but his inspiration was less happy when he took to surrounding his engravings with a design of small grotesque figures. Although Grandville's attacks on the King and his ministers, as well as on the French House of Peers, lacked both bite and style, it was those large, laborious double plates, whose clumsiness was only emphasised by the addition of colour, that were originally held up as examples to his fellow caricaturists. It is curious that Boilly should not have found a place among these. His early

64

Jules Dupré. *Grazing in the Limousin. 1835.* Lithograph

work consisted of engravings in the 18th-century style, but he followed them with *Grimaces*, which achieved considerable success between 1823 and 1828, and were not without influence on Daumier's original productions.

It was in 1832 that there first appeared in *La Caricature* some drawings by an artist who signed himself 'Rogelin' or sometimes just 'Honoré'. So far, the paper, though bold enough in intention, had been somewhat lacking in artistic and comic quality. But Daumier was destined to turn it into a weapon that brought consternation to the 'Establishment' of the day.

Beyond a short apprenticeship in lithography with Ratier, Daumier's only work on stone up to that time had consisted of one or two experiments in the manner of Charlet or Ramelin. But various more savage sketches published in *Silhouette* and elsewhere shortly before the 1830 Revolution *(Mayeux with the Girls, Never mind, to eat all we need is money, With the Nestlings, The Grocer, Blessed are they that hunger and thirst,* and even more *The Old Dragoon, A Hero of July* (1831), showed him, even at the early age of twenty-one, to be a master of satire.

In all probability, it was Philippon who suggested his taking his clay along with him to the Chamber of Deputies and House of Peers, and modelling his thirty-seven little 'busts' from life, instead of working from memory.

HONORÉ DAUMIER. *So this is what we died for.* *c. 1831-35.* Lithograph

Daumier's first caricatures, some full-length and others only head and shoulders, of the judges at the August 1832 trials *(Lameth, Charles de la Motte, Dupin, Père-Scie, Pot de Naz)* show clearly how much they owe to their sculptural origins. They are portraits of individuals, in which the sublime is closely allied to the grotesque, and are characterised by a dynamism hitherto lacking in the work of any of the paper's other contributors. Before many months had passed, Daumier had discovered innumerable and hitherto unsuspected possibilities in the use of stone as a medium. His drawings, 'naturally coloured' as Baudelaire was the first to say of them, no longer needed any artificial heightening, and he was soon able to forego even the use of colour, which Grandville, for example, never abandoned. His earlier plates may have a greyish tone, but he rapidly learnt to make use of every passing or contrasting value and his drawing stands out in a way that shows that, whether working as painter or engraver, he never ceased to look at his subject with a sculptor's eye.

Here at last was the titan needed by Philippon to bring down the pygmy 'Establishment' of the day from its high places; a titan unconscious of his own

HONORÉ DAUMIER. *Men of the Law: a dissatisfied litigant.* *1846.* Lithograph

HONORÉ DAUMIER. *Rue Transnonain. 1834.* Lithograph

strength, still kindly even at his most destructive and distributing his whippings with a smile. He dominated and eclipsed all the smaller fry with whom he was for so long confused.

Generally speaking, it was Philippon who chose the subject and dictated the captions. But this soon ceased to be any restriction for someone with Daumier's abundant vitality. As a caricaturist, Daumier knew how to remain serious and impose his authority even when he was raising a laugh, how to make frivolity itself tell, and how to blow up the slightest incident into an event of monumental proportions.

From 1829 to 1872, with hardly a break, he continued to be the slave of the contemporary scene, though of nothing in the world besides. He produced series after series of lithographs, directed alternately against current morals and current politics, light-heartedly throwing off a body of work even larger than that of either Rembrandt or Goya, the two masters to whom he is most closely akin. *Ministerial Bedlam* and *Pandemonium*, which earned him a term of imprisonment in Sainte-Pélagie, are oblong plates in the Grandville tradition; but Daumier had already surpassed Grandville although his style was still reminiscent of him. These, however, were only the prelude to the great works to be published in the

HONORÉ DAUMIER. *The Growler.* Lithograph

Association mensuelle, founded by Philippon in 1834 in aid of political prisoners, and which included *Le Ventre législatif, Most reverend and puissant brats, Don't rub up against it, Lafayette dished* and *Rue Transnonain.*

It was in *Le Charivari,* the first number of which was issued on 1st December 1832, that *The Drunkard, Big, fat and constitutional,* and *Go to bed Figaro, you are feverish* appeared, as well as many of the early plates showing scenes of every-day life and current morals. *Le Charivari* was responsible for the publication of *Souvenir of Sainte-Pélagie,* as well as of most of the famous series: *French Types, Daytime Pleasures, Robert Macaire, Paris Bohemians, Bathers, Tragi-comic Character Studies, Ancient History, Worthy Citizens, Oarsmen, Married Manners, The Best Days of your Life, The Bachelor's Day, Men of the Law, The Representatives Represented, Divorcées, Vulgar Manners, Parisian Types.* The same paper published most of the *Actualités* which, thanks to Daumier, never belied their title, as well as the series *What more could one want ?* which marked the end of Daumier's flights, once the censorship that followed Napoleon III's *coup d'état* had put an end to attacks on the government. Except for one or two series of grotesques, Daumier's immense output never had the effect of watering down his imagination, nor was he ever reduced to becoming his own imitator.

Obliged to be always right up to date and always pressed for time, he had to adopt increasingly elliptical methods to show movement. The lines along which he developed were similar to those of Titian and Goya, and however dramatic his original drawings, he could always find another dramatic touch to add. Younger at sixty than he had ever been at thirty, he took advantage of every moment of freedom to drop the role of clown to which the public tried to confine him, and took to producing allegorical and symbolic pictures showing a new vein of imagination from which all comic intention was banished. His caricatures gradually gave way to increasingly serious character studies.

Banville paints a vivid picture of him in his *Souvenirs.* 'He used odds and ends of old crayons that could no longer be sharpened, so that he had to invent new angles at which to hold them, with the result that, in his skilled hands, the effect produced was infinitely subtler and more varied than it would have been had he used a new crayon sharpened to a perfect point which would only have broken at the critical moment. I would even say that the breadth and boldness of Daumier's drawing, in which his broad strokes are of the same quality as his shadows and cross-hatching, are due to his habit of using odd bits of crayon.'

Luc-Albert Moreau, in the notes he made for his proposed work on original lithographs, goes with some care into the technique of the man whom he calls the Jupiter of the lithographic Olympus. 'Daumier,' he tells us, 'differed from the other lithographers of the period in not sketching his design on the stone first. He would rapidly jot down, so to speak, a number of lines, forms or shapes, from which a recognisable individual would ultimately emerge. He often touched up his drawings with the pen or the brush, but when he worked only with the pen, without using crayon at all, his work was apt to suffer, as can be seen from the stiff and uninspired set of some sixty plates that he drew for *La*

70

Honoré Daumier. *What more could one want: 2 a.m. leaving the theatre.* Lithograph

ACHILLE DEVÉRIA. *Portrait of Victor Hugo.* *1828.* Lithograph

Caricature. In lithography, Daumier was distinguished by his use of the greasy crayon. He employed all four types of crayon to be found on the market, and what gives such richness and variety to his prints is his frequent repetition of the same type of shading in a single picture. Not for him the inked dabbers used by Engelmann. His flat blacks have, in many cases, been gone over with the scraper as, for example, in *Just as if one were there* of the *Parisian Types*, and many of the *Ancient History* plates. Another method he used to produce deep, velvety blacks full of highlights was to crush his black crayon hard against the stone with an old cork. His way of spraying liquid ink on to the stone with the help of a small brush and a broken-toothed comb shows how much in advance he was of the later poster artists, although Toulouse-Lautrec was to acquire equal skill in the use of spatter. While he managed in this way to produce the most subtle range of greys he was never afraid to slash a picture with great strokes of the scraper, as in his *Return of Ulysses* and *Wrath of Agamemnon*.

'A characteristic of the Daumier technique is the air and light that seem to circulate in his lithographs. In many cases he followed the methods of etching, laying line across line until he achieved the perfect background which he then worked over to bring out the picture he intended. He used these cross-strokes to indicate fluctuation and movement, the shape of the human form, the way clothes cling to the body; then enhanced his blacks and greys by leaving minute areas of untouched white between his hatchings.'

Daumier was no misogynist, but he was apt to be so carried away by ardour for his work as to leave little room for grace, even in series devoted to women such as *Married Manners* or *The Blue-stockings,* even when he penetrated into the country of the gods with his *Ancient History.*

The delineation of the female of the species, with her devilry, her guile and her coquettish airs, Daumier left to Devéria, Gavarni and their like, and to the swarm of lesser artists such as Eugène Lami, Edmond de Beaumont, Wattier, Grévedon, Victor Adam, Andrieux or, later, Grévin, all of whose witty little series of courtly or equestrian scenes must have come as a welcome relief to readers accustomed to the usual bludgeonings of the *Le Charivari*.

Because of the ease with which it slips over the stone, greasy crayon is particularly well suited to produce an effect of gentle, caressing or quivering touch or movement, in which it often surpasses the results achieved by etching. The combined use of crayon and tint enables the artist to suggest the silkiness and brilliance of fine materials. Like their predecessors of the 18th century, French artists under Louis XVIII, as well as under Louis-Philippe and the Second Empire, were part good-natured observers and part artful costumiers. They found infinite interest in the parade of gesture and ornament, the play of light out of doors or inside a room, as well as in love as practised in every imaginable social circle.

Achille Devéria stands head and shoulders above most of the fashionable gossips and chroniclers to whose number he was for so long considered to belong. While his nudes have neither the style nor the disciplined lines of those of Ingres, he surpassed Ingres and all the other great painters of the period in the tenderness with which he could depict young bodies bathed in sun or moonlight. Natural but not trivial, graceful but not mannered, his work rarely became automatic despite the vast quantity he was obliged to produce. By his own virtuosity and with the help of his printer, Motte, he brought the use of colour to a fine art, the beauty of his work being enhanced by the quality of the paper on which it was printed. Devéria's series of engravings such as *The History of a Marriage, Female Types, Twelve Subjects, Modern Taste, Daylight Hours, The Seven Deadly Sins,* etc., are some of the most voluptuous drawings ever made of the instinctive movements of young girls in their own settings, surprised at night or at their first awakening.

This was a period when the portrait-engraving, so beloved of earlier generations, had fallen out of favour and when the writers of the Romantic school were trying to dodge the attentions of artists to whom it would have been an honour for them to sit. But we owe to Devéria some excellent portraits of Victor Hugo, Alfred de Vigny, Lamartine, Alexandre Dumas, Lemercier and Liszt, in their youth, drawn with a sure hand, the likeness sufficiently idealised, the detail adequate without unnecessary flourishes, and all alike vividly alive.

After Henri Monnier, with his *Grisettes,* came Gavarni with his *lorettes,* in creating whom he showed greater wit and charm, besides a far wider appreciation of the possibilities of stone as a medium. In contrast to man, shown as dull, slow and heavy, Gavarni's *lorettes* appear slight, delicate creatures, fully aware of their power, ready to put on any disguise and finding it amusing to dress themselves up as men in order to stress their feminity *(Carnival)*.

Gavarni's early work is somewhat stiff and suffers from the fact that he started life as a fashion illustrator (1830). Soon however, thanks to the influence of Daumier, his lithographs began to show less concentration on minutiae, while his forms gained in depth. He learnt how to enhance the sheen of silks and satins by touches of deep, velvety black on a domino, an apron or a head-dress which themselves take on a richer tone by the contrast. He was himself inclined to melancholy, though he produced so many scenes of gay life, but he lingered on details of dress with the skill and taste of a dress designer and touched in every fold with loving care, while passing more lightly over other details.

'Gavarni and Balzac are a pair, the lithographs of the one are the counterpart of the novels of the other. They are the two great geniuses of the century, neither owing anything to any predecessor.' It is a Goncourt speaking, in *An Artist's House.* The authors of *Woman in the Eighteenth Century* were dazzled by Gavarni, the dandy with his thousand conquests, who slept with a different woman each night and could say such witty things, and who retained his gallant bearing in spite of his prematurely aged appearance. The child-women produced by the artist of the *Invalides de sentiment,* the *Lorettes vieillies* and the simian *Thomas Vireloque,* dressed in pierrot's costume or the clinging trousers of a longshoreman and wholly preoccupied with themselves, were a type to enchant the brothers Goncourt. These plump, useless little creatures, with their delicately arched necks and softly curving bodies, without thought in their heads beyond men and masquerades, nevertheless have something of the fire and roguery of Watteau,

PAUL GAVARNI. *A Private Room at Pétron's.* *1840.* Lithograph

PAUL GAVARNI. *The Brothers Goncourt. 1853.* Lithograph

AUGUSTE RAFFET. *Torchlight Review. 1836.* Lithograph

Fragonard or Lavreince's ladies. Even Goncourt, however, was obliged to admit that Gavarni preferred gossip and the arts of seduction to serious attachment. Fickle as he was, he never looked at a face for long enough to note its distinguishing traits, and flitted from one amusement or entertainment to another, always interested but incapable of feeling real love for any woman.

The admiration for Decamps (1803-1860) which the Goncourts shared with almost every other writer of the period is even less explicable. Being the spoilt child of the critics, Decamps tried his hand at almost everything—watercolours, etching, lithography—and experimented with every kind of subject. Beside those of Delacroix, his Eastern scenes give the effect of tinsel. He was an expert in the training of dogs and monkeys and liked painting animals. Indeed, he was something of a performing ape himself! He had great manual dexterity but his tendency to overdo his effects and his lighting contrasts led him to try to correct the result by tricks of drawing and composition. Nevertheless, he

77

RODOLPHE TÖPFFER. *Landscape with Folly.* Lithograph

has left some plates, such as the *Children frightened by a Dog* and *Caravan at Rest,* which contain more than mere bold design and technical skill and remind us that, among slipshod and trivial works so reminiscent of the contemporary Dutch and Flemish school, he did now and then produce a near-masterpiece such as the *Defeat of the Cimbrians,* today in the Louvre.

Raffet, who died in the same year as Decamps (1860), was genuinely entitled to his popularity. He was the pupil of Gros and Charlet, and inherited and carried on their lyric quality. As André Michel said, Raffet's vignettes can bear enlargement to the size of a large canvas. His *Dream,* his *Waking,* and *They groan but always follow,* produced between 1830 and 1850, transformed the Napoleonic epic into a legend and encircled it with an unearthly light. His pictures are filled with innumerable figures lightly indicated rather than drawn in detail. He makes us hear the menacing roll of the drums, the piercing call of the bugles; he mingles living men with spectres and the rainclouds in the sky are repeated

THÉODORE CHASSÉRIAU. *Venus Anadyomene*. Lithograph

in the clouds of dust underfoot. It is a print of the *Torchlight Review* that Daumier shows one of his *Print Collectors* in the Camondo collection withdrawing from the folder. Unhappily, when he was commissioned to do the two series known as the *Crimean Album* and the *Rome Campaign,* Raffet's inspiration failed him. Instead of the vigour of the military scenes that Guys was producing at the same period, Raffet's series remind us of the official war pictures of a later age, produced in the studio and capable of reducing the most heroic episodes to mere 'accurate records'.

With the exception of Devéria, most lithographers under Louis-Philippe were apt to confine their studies of nudes to somewhat precious imitations of the antique. But Chassériau, who so rarely worked on stone *(Apollo and Daphne),* produced one masterpiece: his *Venus Anadyomene.* The greasy crayon suited his delicate genius far better than the etching needle, and his Venus, one of the most chaste drawings ever made of a woman's form, recalls the work of Correggio or of Leonardo da Vinci. Langourous, a daughter of the sea, her slenderness and pallor recall the same artist's *Esther preparing to meet Ahasuerus.* The latter picture was to haunt Gustave Moreau but he, although he borrowed from Chassériau the same graeco-indian type, distorted it by exaggerating the flesh tints and introducing embellishments more suited to a miniaturist, and a note of decadence characteristic of his period.

In Germany, Senefelder's native country, and Austria, lithography, despite its popularity, inspired no masterpieces. Against a background of generally uninspired work, certain portraits by Shadow, Krüger, Friedrich Jentzen, Feckert, Kriehuber and Lieder stand out. Following the Munich lithographer, Strixner, when the process had just been discovered, Neureuther, Schwind and Menzel usually employed a pen for drawing on the stone. This technique was brought to perfection in Switzerland by Töpffer (1799-1846), a brilliant artist whose folios of comic prints *(Tours in Switzerland, Dr Festus, M. Vieux bois, M. Jabot* and others) entitle him to be called a minor Swiss Rowlandson. His compatriot Calame is one of the rare lithographers who have known how to draw mountains.

The influence exercised on the German humourists by the French caricaturists is plain to see. Dörbeck took Monnier as his model, Hosemann took Grandville, and Pettenkofen, Gavarni. The landscapes of Wagenbauer, Dorner and especially of Achenbach, the follower of Isabey, were also based on French examples.

There was a similar lack of original inspiration in England where, however, Prout and Harding, though not the equals of Boys, are nevertheless in the direct line between Bonington, Boyer and David Robert.

Even in France, lithography seemed suddenly to have exhausted the impetus of its first flowering and to be entering a period of decline, in which it was regarded as no more than a method of reproduction to which photography and heliography would soon be offering serious competition. Artists ceased to provide work for the printers. As a result of the partial abandonment of stone as a medium, in favour of the use of transfer paper and often of transfer on to grained zinc—photo-zincography—clarity of outline was lost. Even Daumier's

PAUL CÉZANNE. *Bathers.* *1898.* Colour lithograph

work suffered from the new techniques and the poor quality of the paper. 'Lithography is a dying art,' lamented Burty in 1867. Truth to tell, in spite of the hitherto unheard of prices reached at the Parguez and Lacombe sales in 1861, very few of those who appreciated lithography really believed in it as a technique. For a long time, it was regarded both in England and America as a poor relation of copper-plate engraving. The very popularity of Daumier's work was the cause of misunderstandings which persist to some extent even today. He is too often commended for his powers as a controversialist and comic artist to the exclusion of the qualities that make him a great master. Many collectors who really prefer work like that of Boilly, Monnier or Decamps have rejected the black-and-white of *Worthy Citizens* or *Men of the Law* in favour of other plates, coarsely coloured by inferior hands.

THE REVIVAL OF COPPERPLATE ENGRAVING IN THE
MID-NINETEENTH CENTURY

It was in 1862 that original engraving received a new infusion of life as the result of a combination of effort of a type hitherto unknown. It is difficult to know exactly how it began or who was its first instigator. It may have been Legros; it may have been Bracquemond. Artists, poets, printers and publishers all joined in a disinterested effort as though they really felt the future of the art to be in danger. Théophile Gautier, Baudelaire and Burty all spoke out in turn while Bracquemond, who had been brought up among printers from his childhood, did his best by spoken word and by writing, without a thought of personal advantage, to stimulate interest in 'mass-produced drawings'. At a time when line-engraving, etching and woodcuts or wood engraving were regarded as useful only for interpreting—or, more frequently, falsifying—the masterpieces of the past, these men were concerned to encourage *original engraving*. They acquired the support of Delâtre, a printer who had been trained under artists, and of Cadart, a publisher whose portrait, engraved by both Desboutins and Ribot, reveals him as a man with the courage to subordinate present success to the joy of fighting for a worthy cause.

The list of the collaborators whom the Société des Aquafortistes collected—or hoped to collect—makes one gasp: Manet, Daumier, Jongkind, Legros, Fantin-Latour, Seymour Haden, Ribot, Whistler, Degas, Pissarro, Puvis de Chavannes, Courbet, Eugène Boudin, together, of course, with others less well known. But all these, though at that time only, for the most part, at the beginning of their careers, were destined to become illustrious names in French painting.

Notwithstanding Bracquemond's own skill as an artist, to which we owe so many charming plates, combining the lessons of Western art with those learnt from Japan (*The Old Cock, The Half-door* or the *Portrait of Edmond de Goncourt*), he chiefly compels our admiration for the widespread influence he exerted in every field, and for his lively brain.

He was behind Théophile Gautier and Baudelaire when the Société des Aquafortistes, which had been founded in 1862, published its first issue, containing *Italian Scene* by Corot and *The Unknown, Golden Plovers* and *Wild Duck* by Bracquemond himself. Of the whole group of engravings that we owe to the collaboration of Delâtre and Cadart, the following may be mentioned especially: *The Sheepfold* by Daubigny, *The Refectory* and *The Riding-school* by Legros, Manet's *Gipsies, View of Maasluis* by Jongkind, *View of the Thames* by Seymour Haden, Hervier's *Boats at Low Tide*, and Ribot's *The Prayer*. Gautier's preface is chiefly remarkable for the way he succeeds in communicating his own enthusiasm to the reader. 'Every etching is an original picture,' he writes. 'To be a successful etcher requires a decision, a sureness of touch and a capacity for visualising the final result that are not necessarily possessed by everyone, however talented and conscientious. There is no room in etching for fumbling or over-elaboration of detail.' In *Le Boulevard*, Baudelaire describes the state into which engraving had then fallen, with the startling precision that characterises all his writing. 'Alas, the discredit and indifference into which the noble art of engraving has fallen is only too plainly to be seen. We can only grasp the splendours of line engraving if we turn back to the works of the past. But there is another art forgotten even more completely than line engraving, and that is etching. In fact, etching, with all its subtlety and magnificence, its depth and naivety, and its light-hearted austerity, in short, its contrasting qualities, has never enjoyed a wide popularity. With the exception of Rembrandt's prints, who is really interested in etching? Who, except a collector, knows anything of the masterpieces produced by the etchers of former ages? The 18th century produced a body of attractive engravings which nowadays lie in dusty piles, selling for a few pence apiece.'

Baudelaire may indeed be said to have shown the way to the Goncourts. Nevertheless, replying to possible critics, he points out the dangers to art that may arise from the careless mistakes and fumblings of artists without a sufficiently assured technique. 'I foresee that there will be many priding themselves on their courage, as others pride themselves on their impetuosity, as being a proof of independence. It is one thing for serious and experienced artists to entrust their drawings or sketches to the public in the form of engravings. They have the right to do so. But the crowd of their imitators may well become excessive. In brief, it must be remembered that etching is a difficult and dangerous art, full of pitfalls, and liable to expose the artist's faults as well as his good qualities.'

Listening to Baudelaire's decisive accents is like listening to the voice of posterity itself, reviewing the works published by the Société des Aquafortistes, singling out as a masterpiece this or that of Meryon's plates, or applauding the publication of Jongkind's *Views of Holland*, Manet's *Portfolios of Etchings,* one or other of Hervier or Daubigny's series, or the *Œuvre unique* of Delacroix.

At the same time, Burty was denouncing the unfairness of academic juries and inviting engravers to form themselves into an independent society, as far removed as possible from official control. He also protested against the danger to wood engraving represented by Gustave Doré and his interpreters who were robbing it of its simplicity, and deplored the decadence into which lithography had fallen and the complete disappearance of line engraving. He encouraged the revival of etching brought about by young artists, although warning them against a certain roughness of technique, constantly emphasising that it was possible 'to combine giving an impression of the whole with a perfectly detailed finish'. His own enthusiasm did not prevent him fearing that within a few years the good in Cadart's publications might have been submerged by the mediocre. He always stressed the skill and individuality possessed by such artists as Whistler, Seymour Haden and Corot, and it was he who, in 1869, invited Manet, Millet, Corot and Jongkind to provide the illustrations for *Sonnets* and *Etchings*.

Cadart's activities were not confined to copperplate engraving and he allowed

FÉLIX BRACQUEMOND. *The Old Cock*. *1882*. Etching

no difficulties to discourage him. In 1868, the *Société des Aquafortistes* changed its name to *L'Illustration nouvelle* and as such continued to appear for the next thirteen years. To the earlier contributors—Jongkind, Bracquemond, Daubigny, Bonvin and Ribot—were now added one or two others of note, such as Buhot and Desboutins. Much the same names appear in the list of contributors to the contemporary publication *L'Eau-forte moderne* (1874-81).

In his famous prefaces, Burty examined the role of the earlier masters of engraving like Delacroix, Barye or Meryon, tried to stimulate public interest by emphasising the beauties of a good print, and dealt in turn with questions such as papers, inks and methods of printing. Unhappily, he was fighting a progressively losing battle. Within a few years, etching had declined into a mere means of mass reproduction for other works by Meryon or Corot; prints were 'touched up' to such an extent that they began to owe more to the tricks of the printer than to the artist himself. Once more, Burty warned against the dangers of over-reliance on the printer's skill. 'Do not talk to me about Rembrandt. Any engraver who prints engravings for which he alone is responsible is continuing to do his own work. It is he who decides what process is to be used. It is quite another thing for an engraver simply to hand over his plate to the printer. Every line that needs to appear in the final print should also appear on the plate and it is mere laziness to expect the printer to give finishing touches that can and ought to be given only by the artist himself.'

There could not be a clearer statement of the perennial argument between those who think an engraving should be printed 'as it stands', and those whose fancy it is to have each print constitute a new work of art, thanks to variations in the inking. The latter concept is only admissible when the artist—a Whistler, a Buhot or a Forain—himself prints his own engravings. Although Bracquemond never actually withdrew his collaboration, he soon ceased to take an active interest in the publications he had helped to found.

Very soon, the artist-engravers grew disappointed and began to turn their efforts in other directions. From 1874 onwards, most of them turned towards the Impressionists, several of whom, like Degas, had experimented privately with engraving but had not contributed to Cadart's publications.

The publication *Du Jour et de la Nuit* which was the dream-child of Degas, Pissarro, Mary Cassatt and Raffaelli, a single number of which appeared in 1880, has left little documentary trace. It included masterpieces such as Degas' *At the Louvre* and Pissarro's *Undergrowth at the Hermitage* but it was killed by public indifference. Had it succeeded, no doubt its contributors would have included Legros, who had in the meantime emigrated to England, Manet, whom the lack of success of his engravings shortly afterwards led to abandon graphic art altogether, and a number of the leading Impressionists such as Renoir, Sisley, Monet or Cézanne. If circumstances had been more favourable, all these would probably, like Pissarro, have felt the fascination of copperplate as a medium. Probably, too, they would have been joined by men like Constantin Guys whose drawings show them to have been potential lithographers or etchers. Not every born engraver recognises the fact. Round about 1880, however, the art of engraving was, as we shall see, at a very low ebb, its only practitioners, apart from **Legros** and **Degas**, being Rodolphe Bresdin and Buhot, and Auguste Rodin whose admirable dry points did not win appreciation until many years later. Such reputation as it still enjoyed was due to the use made of it by Flameng, Jacquemart, Chauvel, Waltner and Ferdinand Gaillard for interpreting other works, the latter, in particular, being a worthy heir of the portraitists of the 17th century.

Such, briefly, was the revival of original etching, which lasted rather more than thirty years. Now it is time to turn back to examine in detail the work of Meryon, Millet, Corot, Whistler, Jongkind and Manet, and the latter's contemporaries Degas, Legros and Bresdin.

ETCHINGS BY MERYON

Many artists, of whom Corot was one, have turned to etching for a distraction but, in spite of producing some brilliant work, have never taken the time fully to master its laws. But the 19th century miraculously produced one artist who was a born engraver and whose production, though not large, equals in quality that of the greatest etchers of his or any other age. This was Meryon, who had no formal training, but whose design is as rigorous as that of the early masters.

Meryon was born in 1821, son of a doctor and of a dancer who died insane. Like Manet, his first ambition was to go to sea. He was a great admirer of Bléry, and taught himself to use copperplate by copying first the works of Karel du Jardin, Salvator Rosa and van de Velde, and later those of the Dutch artist, Zeeman, whose views of Paris led him, between 1850 and 1853, to execute the twenty-two plates dedicated to Zeeman himself. They were issued consecutively and sold at from 25 to 30 francs, but, although shown at the Salon, they awoke no public interest.

Meryon himself considered the *Tourelle, rue de l'Ecole de Médecine* to be his best plate but, in fact, the main body of his work was done before the first attack that necessitated his being put under restraint (1858). His first masterpiece, *The Petit Pont,* appeared as early as 1850, quickly followed by *The Stryge, The Gallery of Notre-Dame, The Clock-Tower, The Pont Neuf, The Pont au Change, The Morgue, The Apse of Notre-Dame.* These showed the difference between him and most of the other topographical engravers whose search after accuracy was apt to make their work dull. Like Piranesi, Meryon succeeded in reaching the heights of his art, and achieved both splendour and simplicity through breadth of vision allied to technical skill.

The rigid control with which he used his etching needle prevented him from falling under the influence of the Romantic school. In a sense, he belonged to that school through his vigour, his passion, and by the contrasts in his urban landscapes in which human beings count for little and the chief movement is supplied by the light. His engravings are filled with a clear though solemn light against which bridges, buildings, towers and spires stand out as though

CHARLES MERYON. *The Gallery of Notre-Dame. 1853.* Etching

CHARLES MERYON. *The Morgue. 1854.* Etching

chiselled, and which gives the stone a patina like that of bronze. Every picture is a reminder of the part played by metal in a work incised on copper with a steel point. The hard, corrosive light in Meryon's etchings is enhanced by his methods of biting.

His prints, which he enjoined should be printed as they stood and without any of the 'touching up' that printers like to give to the flat tones, look as if they had passed through the fire. By some alchemy, the white of the paper seems to throw back an almost golden light while the funereal and almost sodden blacks contrast with the more lightly etched skies and distances. 'The whole problem of etching', wrote Victor Hugo, 'is that of the light and shade in and by itself. M. Meryon solves it magnificently.'

88

CHARLES MERYON *The Petit Pont.* 1850. Etching

Meryon's biographers tell us that he used to work with his plates upright on an easel, his needle held at arm's length like a sword, letting his hand travel slowly upwards from bottom to top. Looking at the preliminary drawings alongside the finished etching, it is easy to see how his inspiration grew as a result of the actual execution, whether it was a question of placing his lines or the process of biting, the latter carried out in the most carefully planned stages.

For this reason, he commanded the admiration both of professional engravers and of painters, over whom, for half a century, especially in England, the influence he exerted amounted almost to an obsession. It is surprising that a man whose art was so masculine and so well-balanced should have given such recurring signs of insanity as, for instance, the subsequent addition of balloons or flocks of crows to the plates of the *Pont au Change* or the *Ministère de la Marine*.

Meryon's interest in detail, in which he resembles Bresdin, never for an instant detracts from the grandeur of his etchings, though it will no doubt be interpreted by psychiatrists as indicating that his views of Paris, unsurpassed for intensity and depth of relief, were done in a state of hallucination. Meryon shows Paris and her monuments *sub specie aeternitatis*. His genius reproduces them for us as they might appear in a dream, unearthly yet with no architectural detail allowed to pass unnoted, despite the fact that they have been so often described that it might have been thought impossible to find any new interpretation to give them.

Burty was the first to draw attention to what might otherwise have escaped notice, namely the liberties taken with reality by Meryon's imagination in his masterpiece *The Petit Pont*. The buildings stand out as though seen by moonlight, but he has not hesitated to make the towers of Notre-Dame impossibly high as seen from the ground. Changes of this kind are allowable in an engraver of genius who, with obvious imperturbability and a skill the reverse of obvious, almost achieves the silence and the splendour of a work by Rembrandt.

JEAN-FRANÇOIS MILLET

It was about the same time, in 1855-56, that Jean-François Millet was also producing his first etchings: *Sewing Woman, Woman churning, Bringing in the Manure, Women gleaning, Men digging, The Evening Vigil, Carding Wool*, and, a few years later, *The Gruel, La Grande Bergère*, and *Leaving for the Fields* (engraved in 1863 for the Société des Dix founded by Sensier). It is easy to imagine the engravings he might have gone on to produce, had the original work of the painter-etchers not met with such complete indifference on the part of the public— despite the Société des Aquafortistes, founded in 1862, to which we will return later.

Dupré once wrote that 'while artists painted on their good and bad days, they never etched except on their good ones,' and this is particularly true of Millet, who was an even greater draughtsman than he was a painter, and whose best qualities were sometimes lost in the complexity and delays of oil-painting. The decision and concision of his engravings are remarkable. It is easy to see that his two chosen masters were Rembrandt, whom he resembles in his seriousness and feeling for light, and Bruegel, from whom he learnt how to give dimension to his forms, and to consider his drawing with the eye of a sculptor.

His full-length figures cling closely to the soil, not only with their sabots but with the weight of their tools—their spades, forks and sickles. The light in which they are bathed does not waste itself in detail nor is it true, as has sometimes been said, that it is apt to lapse into sentimentality; it stresses the great rhythms and draws attention to the design as a whole. 'I was born a peasant,' he used to say, 'and a peasant I shall die.' His wood-cutters, his girls guarding their

JEAN-FRANÇOIS MILLET. *Leaving for the Fields. 1863.* Etching

JEAN-FRANÇOIS MILLET. *The Gruel*. *1861*. Etching

geese or sheep, his labourers, all of whose movements and expression he had noted from a child and whom he used for his 'types', dominate the great plain and its innumerable incidental details. A touch with the dry point is enough to suggest the colour and depth of the sky or the far distance.

The concentration one can feel in Millet, which reflects that of his models, bent on their succession of domestic tasks or on the march of the seasons, gives his engravings (which like Meryon's might almost have been done with a graver) a stoicism that recalls de Vigny. In spite of Millet's own affection for them, there is something stiff in the conventional attitudes of his figures. He once wrote that he would rather say nothing than say it feebly and, in his austerity

JEAN-FRANÇOIS MILLET.   *Peasant Woman emptying a Pail,*   Etching

and scorn of facile charm he often comes near to the Primitives, though he never consciously followed them.

In comparison, Daubigny, whose vast output was spread over the years 1838-1877, appears far less masculine. In spite of his admiration for Ruisdael and Claude Lorrain and the lyric quality that inspired his *Rookery,* his *Sunrise* and his *Spring,* in spite of his feeling for the silvery tones of dawn or moonlight, Daubigny, who shares with Jongkind the title of precursor of the Impressionists, showed in his engravings a certain timidity and a tendency to exaggerate his contrasts.

JEAN-FRANÇOIS MILLET. *Men digging.* *c. 1855.* Etching

COROT AND THÉODORE ROUSSEAU

Although he was, without realising it, one of the greatest etchers of his time, in one sense Corot was not an engraver at all. That is to say, he did his engravings on whatever came to hand—a glass coated with collodion, a copperplate or a transfer paper. He paid no attention to the laws governing a given technique, or to the chemical processes whereby the picture is taken off the plate and reproduced.

It would appear that Corot never visited the printers and had never himself bitten a plate or supervised its printing. He would never make an engraving except at the request of a friend or to occupy a spare moment, and he attached so little importance to those he did make that he never took the trouble to have several of his plates printed at all. This total lack of interest in the art has surprised many engravers, although Bracquemond, who had discovered Corot's earliest plate, *Tuscan Scene* (1845), at the bottom of a tool chest, was not one of them.

As against fourteen etchings, including masterpieces such as *Italian Landscape, Impressions of the Fortifications at Douai* and *The Duomo at Florence,* Corot produced sixty glass prints, done by a process somewhere between etching and daylight printing, many of which pre-date the etchings. In the latter, the needle seems hardly to have brushed the surface of the varnish and yet, in spite of their deceptively casual air, the cross-hatchings carry full conviction. It is they that give the plates their light, irridescent quality, one they share with Claude Lorrain's etchings which they also recall by the relative proportions of the figures and their surroundings. In *Lake with Boatmen* or the *Wooded Landscape,* Corot's

CAMILLE COROT. *Tuscan Scene. 1845.* Etching

THÉODORE ROUSSEAU. *Scree Oaks (in the Forest of Fontainebleau)*. *1861*. Etching

pictures of animals herding round the water, or the calm of the approaching evening, have the same serenity as those of Lorrain. When he introduces human figures into his landscapes, it is only to emphasise the affinity between man and nature.

When they are looked at close to, Corot's etchings appear, as Diderot said of those of Rembrandt, to be a mass of scribbles, but seen from further away, the inner harmony of the design appears, traced by the lightly bitten, intricate lines that seem at first sight so confused. His etchings and those of Jongkind, also a natural engraver, perhaps best typify the evolution that was to take place during the second half of the century in the concept of landscape.

The work of Théodore Rousseau, whose output was even smaller than that of Millet, received considerably less notice than that of the over-prolific Charles Jacques. Rousseau's earlier etchings *(The Edge of the Clearing, Scene in Berry, View from the plateau of Bellecroix)*, his heliographs such as *The Cherry Tree, The*

Plain, The Plant at Biau, and above all his masterpiece on copper, *Scree Oaks* (1861), with its great gnarled tree-trunks and the wonderful effect it produces of the waning light, are as vigorous as any ever produced, and make one regret that his engraved works were so few.

JONGKIND

Jongkind, Delacroix, Daumier and Rodin may be described as some of the most original of the 19th-century engravers. Nevertheless, Jongkind himself only produced twenty-two plates, spread over sixteen years, from 1862 to 1878. The ease with which he worked was apparent from his first *Portfolio of Etchings,* published in 1862, and shows him to have been ready to reproduce on copper-plate any of the innumerable themes his ever alert, though always selective, sensibility and powers of observation seized on throughout his wandering life.

JOHANN BARTHOLD JONGKIND. *Sunset at Antwerp. 1868.* Etching

JOHANN BARTHOLD JONGKIND. *Dutch Scene.* *1868.* Etching

Most of his etchings were done in Belgium and Holland, but another group we owe to his love for the Normandy coast. The Normandy sky, as changeable and beautiful as that of his own country, inspired work which recalls that of Boudin, Cals and Courbet. He found the inspiration for a third group of etchings in the Paris streets. On the other hand, there are no etchings to mark his journeys in the Nièvre or the Midi, or even in the Dauphiné where he ended his days.

In spite of a certain apparent roughness, and a lack of finish due to hasty execution, which have called forth understandable criticism from some of the technical experts, Jongkind's engravings reveal a sureness of touch which cannot be the result of accident. An extraordinary visual memory enabled him, as it enabled Corot, to recollect his emotions from notes taken on the spot.

Jongkind never alluded to his engravings, in his letters or in conversation. It is, however, reported of him that once, when talking to the critic Fourcaud about two of his plates that had disappeared, he said: 'I started by producing

98

this kind of nonsense; but I haven't really gone on with it.' He never worke directly from nature in his engraving, any more than he did in painting. Sometimes his etchings preceded his paintings, as in the case of the pair entitled *Entering* and *Leaving the Port of Honfleur;* sometimes it was the other way about. When working from his original sketches, Jongkind made the necessary transpositions automatically as he exchanged one technique for the other. Not only did he modify the landscape background and the general arrangement, he altered the distribution of light and of tone values and the cloud movements as well. But composition of this kind seems to have been almost unconscious, and never detracts from the sincerity of the whole. It is always the permanent inner values that his interpretation reveals.

It was not by accident that Signac included a reproduction of the *Pont de Six* in his remarkable work on Jongkind's drawings and water-colours. Rembrandt's theme hardly differs at all from one often treated by Jongkind, for example, *Boat at its Moorings*. But the affinities between the two artists are more than superficial; they are fundamental to the mind of each. They resemble each other in their planning, their subordination of detail to the whole, and in the skill with which they obtain the maximum effect with the fewest lines.

It has to be admitted that cleanliness was not among the honest Dutchman's most striking qualities. As is well known, he painted with anything that came to hand, with the handles of his brushes as readily as with the bristles, while his colours were not infrequently blended with the droppings of the pigeons flying round his canvas. He showed the same lack of care in his engraving, which is full of examples of cracked varnish, splashed acid and lines where his needle has slipped. He did not even take the trouble to reverse his signature and, if his lines are examined under the magnifying glass, they are revealed as odd, chaotic and irregular. Sometimes they look like cross-hatchings but even so there is no regularity. They look as if his hand had been unsteady—as, indeed, drink sometimes made it. But, despite this, it never failed in its obedience to the slightest impulse, as to the most imperious command, dictated by a singularly acute vision. The method of drawing for which students of Rembrandt have tried to find a name, which consists in replacing straight lines by loops, coils and zigzags, occurs in all Jongkind's work. He also used the same angular, broken lines as Daumier, by which he achieves the same incredible variety in depth and intensity. What Delacroix described as 'that monstrosity, the straight line' has no place in his work, even for marking a horizon. Jongkind is anxious to remind us that the earth is round. There was never an artist more naively arbitrary, nor one who, in defiance of the teachings of the schools, knew better how to enhance a value or make the white of the paper vibrate against shadows heightened to produce the full effect.

Not only Jongkind's figures, but even his inanimate objects (even one might say, the planes of his engravings) possess an extraordinary intensity of expression and movement. Earth and sky seem partners in an action filling the whole picture up to the horizon, and continuing to left and right without apparent limits.

ALFRED SISLEY. *Geese.* *1897.* Colour lithograph

The best example of all is the *Sunset at Antwerp,* especially the first state. The later states have not actually been altered; as in the case of most etchings the difference between them consists only in the addition of minor touches; but the blacks of the first print are clean and light, as against the muddy blacks of later printings. In the foreground, on the left, there is a boat. Behind that, a three-masted vessel is outlined against the sky with another ship in full sail nearby.

In the background there is the coast. The sun is sinking and there is a kind of light mist clinging to the leaves of the trees and veiling the church spires. It is a plate that captures all that is best in the art of the Impressionists. What gives it its miraculous quality is the way in which the light vibrates through the forms, breaking up and transfiguring them. Seen from close to, it is an inextricable maze, like a tangle of fine hair; but moving back one is startled by the precision shown in the smallest lines, the perfectly calculated placing and depth of each. In some places, there is an incisive line that leaves the copper bare; in others, the merest trace drawn across the varnish. The water, opaque yet as transparent as air, reflects a thousand points of light, concentric circles spreading out from a speck of pure gold; its movements seem repeated in the clouds overhead. Part of the beauty of this masterpiece of 19th-century engraving comes from the subject itself, but the same qualities are evident in views such as *Maasluis, Entering* and *Leaving the Port of Honfleur*, as well as in *Demolition in the rue Saint-Marcel* or *Gateway of the Hôpital Cochin*, with their atmosphere of wintry cold, poverty, and old, decaying buildings, and which express, perhaps for the first time, the emotions aroused by barren landscapes, all stone-greys and muddy-browns, under scudding clouds or angry sunsets, rich with colour.

JOHANN BARTHOLD JONGKIND. *Leaving the Port of Honfleur. 1863.* Etching

ALPHONSE LEGROS. *Portrait of a Man.* Etching

LEGROS AND RIBOT

Millet's own works were never destined to capture the public at large, but another artist was to find in them the inspiration he needed to produce engravings of great originality which, however, won so little recognition in France that he was obliged in the end to seek it elsewhere. Alphonse Legros was not of peasant stock, like Millet, but he had lived close to the soil, and known from his childhood the meaning of poverty. Throughout his life, he remembered the country ways, the homely rites of work and mealtimes, as strictly observed as those of worship. He was also deeply versed in the greatest work of the past, and he had a strong visual memory, which was fostered in him by Lecoq de Bois-baudran.

His deep, widely-spaced hatchings and the severity of his style remind us of Millet, whose work he had studied with close attention. The lines of his drawing are generous, careful and deliberate. But while Millet's plates speak of work and resignation, Legros' more romantic side expressed itself in tragic scenes in which man is shown at grips with destiny and facing huge cataclysms. He was haunted by the idea of death, which Delacroix thought of only in terms of Shakespeare and Millet in terms of a fable by La Fontaine. Without equalling Daumier, whose art was less consciously devised, or Rembrandt—whom he nevertheless sometimes recalls by the underlying sadness of some of his land-scapes or the faces or hands of some of his figures—Legros is yet far removed from the prettiness and the easy emotion cultivated by later artists. His engravings are great enough to need no incidental enhancements. He always advised his pupils to show boldness, to be prompt in attack and rapid in exe-cution.

Those are the qualities that stand out in all his own work and to which it owes its beauty, no matter whether the engraving is light and delicate, or full of dramatic contrast. His skill in biting his plates was unrivalled, and no one ever supervised this most important stage with greater care. In his simple, assured design, a light background will be used to emphasize the strength of the main outline while the subdued tones produced by the dry point contrast with the clear-cut lines of etching. Whether he is drawing figures or landscape, the simpler his technique the greater the effect it produces. His learning, as much as his passionate interest in individual character made him, with Ingres and Gaillard, one of the best portrait-engravers of the century, as witness his *Cardinal Manning, Dalou, Edwin Edwards* or his *Poetic Ecstasy* or *Spanish Beggar.* The combination of thought and emotion that characterised Legros, and in which he was akin to the Primitives, found its best expression in his portraits. Beside them, the best work of Desboutins or Zorn seems superficial and exaggerated. Legros did some charming and thought-ful work with gold-and silver- point, but he was essentially an engraver and his work on copper surpassed anything else he ever did. His full worth is still not realised in France, although in the course of some fifty years he produced nearly eight hundred pictures.

Théodule Ribot (1823-1891), steeped in the work of Rembrandt as well as of the Spanish school, deserves to be better remembered for his small interiors, figures and still-lifes, which are full of honesty and vigour. He was as apt to use a knitting needle or kitchen knife as his graver, and he often allowed the acid to eat into his varnish; but this only added to the force of his deeply incised lines and great, sweeping hatchings, lightened occasionally by a touch of aquatint. It was skill, not artifice, that taught him his use of chiaroscuro whereby he concen-trated all the light in a picture on the faces or hands of the figures.

RODOLPHE BRESDIN.　*Death's Jest Book.*　Etching

Contemporary with Meryon, and an equally solitary figure, Rodolphe Bresdin, whose life was no less unusual than his character, devoted all his talents to graphic art.

We have little information on his birth or training and what little we know is further obscured by the contradictory evidence of writers whose interest lay largely in the oddities of his character. His earliest work dates from 1839, when he was seventeen, some examples being no larger than a postage stamp. The story goes that 'Chien-Caillou' produced his engravings with the help of a shoebrush and polish and sold them to junk shops for a few francs. By 1848 he was in Toulouse, where he was lithographing *The Good Samaritan,* living in a kind of stable which he shared with a company of birds, cats and rabbits. In moments of sadness, he would end his letters: 'Your friend, despite rain and wind'. The year 1869 found him in Paris; his sight was going and it seemed as though he was done for. Then, in 1876, after he had dropped completely out of sight, he suddenly turned up again one fine day, in a café, hung around with parcels and followed by a wife, six children and a negro. He had achieved his ambition, to emigrate to the New World, but all he found there was disappointment. Later he was given a job on the upkeep of the roads round the Etoile, whereupon he settled down in the centre of Paris in an attic which, to the horror of the other tenants, he transformed into an orchard complete with real springs of water. In 1885, after having been reduced to selling the produce of his little garden in the market as his only means of livelihood, he died at Sèvres from pneumonia, in the great deal bed he had made for himself.

These picturesque details make it easier to understand his work. Whatever Bresdin's contacts with Paris life, modern art seems to have completely passed him by. He continued, at least mentally, to live alone in solitary spaces. The novels of Fenimore Cooper gave him, besides his self-chosen nickname, the illusion of being free, far from civilisation; his thatched huts with their colonies of birds, his uncultivated gardens, his rabbits, tree-frogs and spiders are the real clues to his art.

Bresdin was never tired of repeating that 'the real artist ought not even to look at nature', a surprising reaction on the part of a man obsessed with the idea of patience, who found his amusement in numbering roofs of distant towns, blades of grass in a field, the branches in a forest, the fissures in rocks or the wrinkles on the face of sky or water. Incapable of drawing from life, he made for himself a precarious retreat in which he was able to build up a world peopled by his obsessive imagination with marching legions, fleeing tribes, hermits, Holy Families and all the animals of creation. He had only to look at a bush or wall for it to take on a sudden fantastic life which he successfully communicates to us. In his imagination he saw forests of lances, peoples as numerous as ants, women in long veils or turbans, anchorites, unicorns, thousands of towers or minarets pushing up into the sky.

Some of his engravings, in their degree of fantasy, recall Hieronymus Bosch,

Rodolphe Bresdin. *The Peacocks*. *1869*. Etching

RODOLPHE BRESDIN. *Nymphs bathing.* Etching

Altdorfer, the elder Bruegel, or even Callot. But Bresdin could create his own mystery without need for either the baroque or the macabre. The beauty and the grandeur of his art come from his use of familiar forms, the contrasts of light and shade and the whole mystery behind the outward appearance. It is as though he had looked at the world through a magnifying glass, and it is only if we also look as closely into his compact landscapes that we shall discover the innumerable beauties they contain. Such a mass of detail can be exasperating in other artists; with Bresdin, in contrast to the puerile race of miniaturists, the object of all this precision is to reveal infinity. He never loses the sense of the whole when building up his microcosm. In all his best pictures, such as *The Good Samaritan,* his *Holy Families,* the set in the *Revue Fantaisiste, The Peacocks, Death's Jest Book,* it is a world in travail that is breathing and changing before our eyes. Extraordinary analogies appear between different species; despite the profusion of detail every inch of every picture is alive.

Bresdin never varied his technique, whether he was etching or lithographing. Each plate is covered with a myriad little points, finer than the finest grain of aquatint, and the delicacy of his niello-work makes it easy to understand how he wore out his sight. The 'Gros-Caillou's Calvary' continued and he 'bore his stone' to the end. At sixty years of age he was still consoled by the same visions and his last etching, in which all his themes reappear once more, is entitled *My Dream*.

DEGAS

Edgar Degas was not one of Cadart's team and it is almost certain that his engravings, which he rarely exhibited and which were known only to a few friends like Rouart, Lerolle, Bracquemond and Mary Cassatt, exercised little or no influence. It was the sales that took place after his death that revealed the first part of a body of work formed almost exclusively of portraits. Degas belonged to the same generation as Manet, and had his first etching bitten in 1856, when he was twenty-one. It is a half-length self-portrait. Up to that time, with the exception of Ingres' *Pressigny*, 19th-century etching had included very few portraits. The careful cross-hatchings on the first state of Degas' plate show us how far he was still under the influence of the classic tradition. He was as often to be found in the Print Room as in the galleries of the Louvre. The number of states that exist of each of his engravings are evidence of a mind always searching for perfection. This first attempt shows him to have been not only an admirable draughtsman ('I was born to draw,' he used to say) but a born engraver, for whom etching was a means of expression that imposed its own rules. The first state of his self-portrait is light and only slightly bitten. It was followed by a succession of fresh bitings, each state being worked over with the dry point and burnisher until a sensitive background was produced, thus altering the whole appearance of the plate and making it a study in light and shade.

His biographers give no due to the identity of the person from whom he learnt engraving. It may perhaps have been Tourny, of whom he did a portrait in Rome the following year. But his real master was Rembrandt whose work he copied *(Young Man seated in thought)* and whose influence is clearly to be seen in the little portrait of his father. There are several other etchings that also show the immense and passionate care he lavished on interpreting individual character and expression. These are traditional works in the best sense of the term; ageless and independent of external detail.

One day, when Degas was copying Velásquez's *Infanta* at the Louvre straight on to copper, without making a preliminary drawing, Manet came up and exclaimed at such boldness, adding that he himself would never dare attempt such a thing. We have few details of the friendship that was later to develop between these two artists, each of whom was to influence the other. Both of them found an adviser in Bracquemond. The three half-length portraits of Manet, showing him seated, with his hands crossed, or holding a top hat, date from 1864. In the first, Degas followed Manet's frequent habit of using grain. The three,

EDGAR DEGAS. *Self-portrait.* *1855.* Etching

taken together, show in the natural attitudes the skill with which a movement is caught, and the freer line, how Degas' style was developing. His charming *Marguerite de Gas* (1865) might seem to herald a return to a more classical manner, did not the treatment of the sleeve in the foreground already hint at the originality that would distinguish his later work.

It is impossible to exaggerate the interest presented by this group of portraits to which, after a gap of ten years, Degas added the plate he called *At the Louvre*. This work is of capital importance, not only on account of the originality of the composition but because it is possible to trace its progress through twenty different states, and to see how the general design, perspective and even the distribution of light and shade, were modified by the successive additions of grain and the use of the burnisher. It is eloquent of the thirst for perfection that made Degas write that no art was less spontaneous than his own.

Whereas Manet hardly modified his etchings at all, Degas and Pissarro are the only two artists of their generation who have left us so many states of each etching that we can follow the progress of their continual efforts to enrich their original design.

In about 1875 appeared Degas' first *Dancers*, for which he used a combination of dry point and light grain, employing the burnisher in much the same way as lithographers do the scraper. His blacks show an infinite variety, while his whites (music hall lights, dresses dazzlingly white under the arc lamps, the reflection of lamps or gas jets on ironing tables) are enhanced by the use of roulette, soft ground and aquatint. 'For Degas,' writes Paul Lafond, 'engraving was a distraction and a means of expressing his thought; not just a method of interpreting his paintings. He used every kind of formula and technique, every kind of 'trick', some well-known and common enough, others less known or long since abandoned. He had only to hear of a new tool to adopt it. He used the soft ground that had almost vanished for three-quarters of a century, stopping-out varnish, sulphur, glass-paper, brushes, grain, and various shapes of point. He could not leave his plates alone but was always re-touching them, working them over, subjecting them to a series of successive bitings. He was no less fascinated by inks and papers.'

Lafond is justified in using the word 'trick', but ingenuity of that kind is allowable when, as was the case with Degas, it is made the servant of inspiration. Then it can fairly be described as evidence of conscientiousness and lack of arrogance; a desire to find a way round difficulties. Degas always aimed at something more than external effects and picturesque detail. Paul Jamot summed him up admirably when he wrote: 'His search after new forms of composition and new lighting effects was simply one of his tools of trade.'

As his skill grew, his drawing became more composed. He began trying to catch forms in movement and suddenly gave free rein to a violence hitherto restrained. He had come a long way from the careful portraits of his earlier period. It was not, however, that he was now more easily pleased; on the contrary, the number of states increased. As we have seen above, we have twenty states for *At the Louvre,* eight for the *Dancers in the Wings,* thirteen for *After*

EDGAR DEGAS. *At Les Ambassadeurs. c. 1875.* Etching

the bath. At a time when it was fashionable to 'debunk' Degas and to compare him unfavourably with Manet and Lautrec, Paul Jamot wrote: 'The ideas usually came from Degas; he thought up the subjects and his friends profited by them.' What Jamot said of the paintings applies equally to the engravings: 'It was Degas' privilege to treat subjects that had hitherto only attracted *genre* painters. Not the least unusual or least valuable of his achievements is to have succeeded in transforming *genre* engraving by bringing to it an inspiration and a depth worthy of the finest creations of the great novelists.'

Despite the fact that Manet, like Corot, never considered engraving as of other than secondary importance, leaving it to friends or printers to arrange for the biting or publication of his work, and although he never seems to have taken the time to master its technique, his slightest engraving shows such power and decision that even professionals are forced to admire the work of an amateur whose knowledge was acquired by instinct and who, like other great painters, never found time 'to learn the rules'.

Like Courbet, Manet worked mostly with the brush; his larger works were rarely preceded by more than the most summary of sketches, and drawing, for him, hardly ever constituted an end in itself. In the same way, engraving remained for him a side-line. A great artist is great in every field. To study Manet's etchings and lithographs is to learn his character, follow his development and appreciate how he came to exert the influence he did.

Even from his admirers, however, he does not seem to have met with much encouragement in his engraving. Although he issued a first collection of etchings in 1862, Baudelaire only mentions it incidentally and it was long before it was appreciated at its real value. The list of his works issued in 1906 shows the number of plates remaining unpublished at his death to have been almost equal to the number published, their very existence, in many cases, being unsuspected until revealed in the collections of Bracquemond, Burty, Degas and Guérard. Manet's contacts with printers were few and far between, nor was he particularly interested in technical processes. It is the more surprising, therefore, that he should, from the first, have been attracted to the complicated art of etching, and it may be he would never have been so but for the work of Goya. He most probably regarded it as a simplified method, offering an easy way of producing contrasts of light and shade.

The Gipsies, which he produced at the age of twenty after a painting that he later destroyed, as well as the plates in his first collection of etchings, show Manet not to have worked directly from the model in his engraving but to have interpreted, often very freely, his own paintings *(The Guitarist, The Absinthe-drinker, Gamin, Espada, Little Girl,* etc.) or of various masterpieces of the Spanish school *(Horsemen, Philip II,* etc.). This explains the somewhat lifeless, studied aspect of certain of his engravings. Their air of having been made up in the studio contrasts with the freedom and vigour of the drawing of his original productions when he is not working from an earlier composition.

Does Manet deserve to be placed, as Léon Rosenthal placed him, among the 'dynamic' masters such as Rembrandt, Rubens, Delacroix, Daumier or Degas? He possesses neither their memory nor their sense of movement. His figures do not lack life but they are almost always motionless, either sitting or standing. While the similarity between him and Goya cannot be ignored—*Exotic Flower* is a complete pastiche of *Bellos Consejos*—it is due less to affinities in their temperaments and choice of subject than to the fact that Manet learnt his art from studying *Los Caprichos.* He follows the same technique of little, short, parallel

EDOUARD MANET. *Christ with Angels*. *1864*. Etching

strokes, sensitive and without cross-hatchings, that bring the backgrounds to life and that Canaletto had used before Goya. He incises his plate deeply in order to produce a clean, vivid line. His firm use of the point, which produces his rich blacks and intense whites, is combined with great delicacy of drawing. One has only to look at *La Toilette,* an admirable engraving which, for an instant, calls up a faint memory of Chassériau, to see how certain areas are scored across with long parallel lines as in Rembrandt; or the second state of *Olympia* in which the dead white of the body and the opaque black of the background are contrasted with the almost Venetian sheen of the silks.

The most simply engraved of his plates, that owe nothing to either aquatint or the advice of technical friends such as Bracquemond or Guérard, are perhaps the most significant. Such are *The Baïlarin, The Philosopher* (in which the bearded face, black hat and body draped in its cape stand out against the shifting lines of the background), the engraving of *Rouvière playing Hamlet, Child with a Sword,*

EDOUARD MANET. *Lola de Valence. c. 1862.* Etching

FERDINAND GAILLARD. *Dom Prosper Guéranger.* *c. 1885.* Line engraving

and the extraordinary *Queue at the Butchers*. The latter plate, discovered after the artist's death, should no more be regarded as a final piece of work than the various drawings after Eva Gonzalès or Berthe Morisot. Nevertheless, by its very sketchiness, it shows Manet to be, not merely 'a traditional executant of the first rank'—the phrase is Geffroy's—but a precursor in the true sense of the word. The forms are suggested merely by a series of little, parallel hatchings, the masses seeming in many places to have been swallowed up in light. Manet was the first engraver—and in this respect his work was far more revolutionary than that of Whistler, Degas or Pissarro—to follow the Impressionists in moving towards that 'complete disintegration of the forms through light that leads to the suppression of contour.'

Generalisations based on plates that have remained at the stage of preliminary sketches are better avoided, but many of Manet's etchings and, as will later be seen, of his lithographs as well, show a definite attempt—probably under the influence of the Japanese and Degas—to substitute for the immobile attitudes and 'local form' (if the phrase may be allowed as a counterpart to 'local colour') of his earlier work, the unexpectedness belonging to shapes distorted and disintegrated by conflicts of all kinds.

LINE ENGRAVING AND FERDINAND GAILLARD

It took a long time for critics or collectors to accept anything but line engraving as being worthy of their attention. As late as the end of the 19th century, as the sales of prints bore witness, most of the big collections were only interested in *tours de force* achieved by experts in technique who thought they had the right to interpret masterpieces, even though they themselves possessed no talent and did not consider the rules interpretations should follow worth a thought. The innumerable line engravings *à la* Calamatta produced about this time and, as it were, under the hypnotic influence of Ingres, look as if they had one and all come from the same workshop and were products of the same uninspired manufacturing process. The interpreters were incapable of individuality and just fit to reproduce a Meissonier or a Roybet where no question of spoiling a masterpiece could arise.

In 1868 a Society was founded at the *Gazette des Beaux-Arts* to encourage reproductive engraving. Not unnaturally, the founder was Henriquel-Dupont who was regarded at the Ecole des Beaux-Arts, where he taught copperplate engraving, as something of an innovator. He had to some extent brought about a revolution by combining the use of the graver with that of the point and varying the placing of his lines to avoid too much monotonous regularity. He had also produced one or two striking portraits. His prestige succeeded, for a time, in arresting the decline of a technique which was soon to receive its death-blow as a result of improvements in photo-mechanical processes of reproduction. The efforts of the *Société des Graveurs au burin* to protect the interests of

PAUL SIGNAC. *The Buoy*. Colour lithograph

its members by arranging a succession of exhibitions were destined to be in vain. They were trying to perpetuate a technique that was already an anachronism, despite the fortunes lavished on keeping it alive. (As much as 5,000 or 10,000 francs were paid for some plates, enormous sums for that period.) In his *Journal*, Eugène Delacroix had already denounced people 'who were trying, in their own way, to make a name for themselves by exhibitions of technical expertise that only succeeded in diverting attention from the picture itself.' 'The language of the engraver', he once said, 'does not consist simply in imitating the effects of painting, which is a different language altogether. Engraving has its own language which the engraver, if his interpretation of the original work is a faithful one, can use to express his own feelings.' Bracquemond was never tired of saying the same thing. He was a great opponent of the contemporary methods in teaching engraving and held that engravers who put line before everything else were responsible for the deplorable amount of undistinguished work produced. 'We have only one studio and one engraver: the Institute,' he wrote. 'In the prints produced by the early engravers who worked under the great masters, the lines never cover the whole surface of the paper, because this, for the engraver, is his source of light. But engravers who have learnt their art in the schools regard line as so important that they scatter lines everywhere. The tone of a Rubens, engraved by one of them, is exactly the same as that of any indifferent picture by any third-rate artist.'

Of all the anonymous crowd of engravers who had for years been covering copperplates with their dreary, regular hatchings, Bracquemond singled out only one. This was Ferdinand Gaillard, and what distinguished him was that he was a great draughtsman.

He was a remarkable figure, this Franciscan strayed into the modern world. Whether interpreting *La Gioconda, Man with a Carnation* or *The Journey to Emmaus,* he made the picture part of himself and, at the cost of infinite work and struggle, enriched it with his own inspiration. From his preliminary sketches, we can see how he analysed first the whole picture, and then the detail of its shadow and contours. He even used statues or the living model when studying a painting, to ensure that he had grasped its full meaning before setting down to reproduce not just its outward shape but its spirit with his graver. Not since the old masters had an artist known how to put himself on one side, for the sake of the work, in the way of this brother of the Third Order of St Francis. It might almost appear as though line engraving had selected him on purpose to sing its swan-song. In every one of his plates, Gaillard shows a care in finding ways of suggesting colour and transposing the values without distorting them that almost entitles him, even in his reproductive engravings, to be called an original engraver in his own right.

Gaillard most faithfully interpreted Van Eyck, Donatello, Raphael or Rembrandt, but it was only too rarely that he allowed his own personality to emerge more fully. Then his skilful, modest technique revealed him as a man belonging at once to his own and to every age. His portait engravings of *Dom Prosper Guéranger, Sister Rosalie, Pius IX* and *Leo XIII* are among the most

moving ever made. Their beauty comes from the depth and sincerity of the artist's own feelings, and the emotion they arouse is never dulled by the somewhat complex treatment which he might almost have imposed on himself as a further discipline or mortification. For some of his engravings he did as many as thirty states, and into each he put so much work that one wonders how, in a century when etching was making such strides, anyone could have continued to use the graver to make all those thousands of dots and closely incised lines. It seems a miracle that the spirit should nowhere be sacrificed to the letter, the feeling to the execution, or the whole to the detail. In Gaillard, as Béraldi said, line is truly the means and not the end.

Today it needs a real effort to be fair to art of this kind, and not to be put off at first sight by some of the plates with their engraved surrounds, in imitation of Nanteuil, that to our eyes look so old-fashioned. A superficial observer, not noticing the depths of light and shade, the contrasts and the perspective, and blind to the fire behind them, might dismiss Gaillard as dull and spiritless.

But the reflection and anxious care with which he approached his work never for an instant quenched his inspiration, as witness the first versions of *Dom Prosper Guéranger* or *Sister Rosalie* in which parts of the plate have been so incised that they resemble an old piece of worm-eaten timber. His method was anything but systematic; and he would use burin, scraper, burnisher, hammer and dry point all in turn. Through the series of states, it is possible to follow his different moods—hesitant, violent, contradictory—and to detect his second thoughts. In a first state, the head often looks as though modelled by a sculptor, the character or signs of old age clearly marked. Then progressively he begins to build up the expression, softening the contrasts, linking one detail to another, giving to the humblest face some reflection of the divine. Sometimes he began with a wealth of detail that he subsequently eliminated—what he called his 'drops of water method'; elsewhere the great, decisive lines came first. His familiarity with every process of engraving meant that he did not hesitate to combine them all in a single plate, and his perfect knowledge of how best to use each brought results that were undreamed of by his predecessors.

ETCHING IN ENGLAND, BELGIUM AND GERMANY
SEYMOUR HADEN, WHISTLER, LEYS, BRAEKELEER

English engraving had hitherto been shackled by a multiplicity of rules and traditions. But now two artists, as it happened related to each other, were to stimulate new interest in painters' engraving, an art which has nothing in common with engraving as practised by the virtuosi of portraits, historical scenes and hunting prints. The influence of these two was to be further strengthened by that of Legros when he later emigrated to London.

Between 1857 and 1897, Seymour Haden (1818-1910), with the encouragement of Whistler, executed nearly two hundred plates, though of quite a different type from those of his brother-in-law. He was a great admirer of Rembrandt, and made a special study of his engravings, the authenticity of some of which he contested. Rembrandt was always his best guide and he followed him in subjecting his plates to successive bitings, with additions in dry point. His work is more lively than that of Whistler, though it lacks Whistler's charm and sensibility. Some plates, for example *Springtime in Ireland*, while recalling the work of Daubigny, also anticipate the Impressionists, Haden having been, in his own way, an innovator. The sure touch apparent in all his landscapes, most of them showing the banks of the Thames or the countryside round London, and his strength and sincerity, contributed largely to the emancipation of the English school of engraving. Even today, it bears traces of his influence, along with that of Meryon, Whistler and Legros.

James McNeill Whistler was born in America in 1834 and spent his working life between London and Paris. Like all the great artists of his generation, his work was refused for the Salon and condemned by the critics. From his early days he was the friend of Fantin-Latour (who put him in the foreground of his *Homage to Delacroix* and in *Toast*), Courbet, Baudelaire, Bracquemond and Legros, who realised at once that he was destined to become an engraver without rival, and for this reason he is often claimed by the French school.

Vehement and impulsive, he was more at his ease in smaller pictures done at a single sitting, than in larger works such as his full-sized portraits or his *Nocturnes*. Not only his *Paris, Thames, Venice* and *Amsterdam* sets, which he engraved directly on the copper, but also his lithographs with their delicate ash-grey tones (p. 203-4) as light as the Japanese butterfly he used as signature, are little miracles of sureness and concision, characteristic of his acute and well-informed mind.

As he gained in experience, he abandoned the over-minute technique of his earlier work, and searched for a freer, more spontaneous style of composition. All his later work, portraits, interiors and city scenes, as well as landscapes, shows him to have relied increasingly on the freshness of first impressions, rather than on memory.

JAMES McNEILL WHISTLER. *Venice: S. Maria Salute at Dawn.* *c. 1880.* Etching

JAMES McNEILL WHISTLER. *View of the Thames. 1859.* Etching

Whistler was one of the first to take his plates with him and engrave direct, without making any preliminary sketch, in the open air. He was also one of the very few engravers, before Manet, to aim at capturing impressions and reproducing on stone or copper the finest vibrations of inanimate, as well as of living, subjects.

In his first set of *Twelve Etchings from Life*, the so-called 'French set', printed by Delâtre in 1859 and dedicated to Seymour Haden, portraits alternate with landscapes. In the same year in Paris, as though to show that he was not intimidated by Meryon's achievements, he published *The City* and followed it up by a second series entitled *Sixteen Views of the Thames* (Black Lion Wharf, Rotherhithe, etc.) which recall Baudelaire's description, written after seeing the exhibition of Whistler's collected prints at the Galerie Martinet of 'a marvellous tangle of rigging, sails and ropes; furnaces and swirling smoke seen through an enveloping mist; all the profound and elaborate poetry of a vast capital.'

Especially in his further sets of London, Venice and Holland done after 1864, it is possible to trace an increasingly selective summariness, due to the influence both of Japanese art and of Canaletto. What contemporary opinion regarded as little more than unfinished sketches are now seen to be true masterpieces in

123

JOSEPH PENNELL. *The Offices of 'Punch'.* Etching

ADOLPH FRIEDRICH MENZEL. *Studies for 'The Asylum'. 1844.* Etching

which the sensitivity of the biting produces an effect of mingled gaiety and reflection. Whistler subsequently took to doing his own printing of these, and his variations in inking sometimes produce almost the effect of aquatint.

The four hundred plates he produced between 1858 and his death in 1903 testify to his increasing receptivity and the variety of his themes, from the charming portraits of *Fumette, Finette, Maud, Tillie, La Mère Gérard* or the sculptor Drouet—all done before he was thirty, at the same period as the *Street in Saverne, Beggar's Soup* and the *Forge*—to the *Naval Review at Spithead, Dance-hall* or the series of Chelsea shops.

Whistler has left his own account of what he considered etching should be. 'The space to be covered should always be in proper relation to the means used for covering it. In etching, the means used, or instrument employed, being the finest possible point, the space to be covered should be small in proportion... ...The huge plate, therefore, is an offence... There should be no margin on the proof.' Elsewhere, he took occasion to remind those who judged a picture by the amount of earnest labour that it showed, that the test of a good picture was that it did not suggest any effort on the part of the artist.

ADOLPH FRIEDRICH MENZEL. *The Last Treasure.* *1895.* Etching

GUSTAV KLIMT. *Portrait of a Woman. 1896.* Lithograph

Towards the end of his life, it may be that Whistler's violent reaction against over-elaborate technique and his attempt to reproduce nothing but the essence of what he saw occasionally led him to the brink of affectation. But that is apt to be the price one has to pay in art for too much sensibility. His influence continued to be felt in France and in England, where it is especially evident in the work of artists such as Edwin Edwards, Sir John Charles Robinson, Cameron, Heseltine, Strang and Joseph Pennell. One valuable result was to stimulate young engravers to aim at something more than being deliberate imitators of Meryon, and induce them to turn back for their subjects to the homely sights of the countryside, or small, carefully observed scenes like those popularised by James Tissot, Frenchman by birth and Londoner by adoption, whose pictures of elegant English life have a vivacity of line not unlike that of Helleu.

The German states and the Low Countries, which had been the birthplaces of original engraving, produced nothing of any note during the first half of

WILHELM LEIBL. *Portrait of the painter Hortig.* Etching

the 19th century. In Belgium, the only exception was Baron Leys (1815-1869) who lived and died in Antwerp. His prints of historic scenes, like the *Institution of the Order of the Golden Fleece* and *Luther reading,* were much admired by Burty for their rugged sincerity and restraint. Today their romanticism seems somewhat faded.

H. de Braekeleer (1840-1888) left eighty plates, all of which he printed himself. He came at first under the influence of Leys but soon abandoned dramatic reconstructions of historical scenes for landscapes and views of Antwerp, together with a series of poignant little sketches of men and women at work *(The Coppersmith, The Lace-maker, The Clothes-mender),* members of his own family, or poverty-stricken little houses or street stalls which in their intensity and depth of feeling already look forward to the work of Ensor and Van Gogh.

'The German school', wrote Count Delaborde in his study of engraving published in 1835, 'does not lack skill but suffers from the limitations it imposes on itself by a kind of narrow obstinacy. It is still a slave to the tyranny of line and the classical style it favours stifles all imagination. This is not to deny the value of the idealistic principles that have governed German art since the time of Overbeck and his disciples, whose original movement was more than justified by the abuses of the previous century. But though their ideals are worthy of all respect, doctrinaires like this fall down in practice. They seem to think the only object of engraving is to produce a simple outline on the plate with the possible addition of one or two weak shadows. Their lines are hard but there is no crispness about them and they have no life.' There could hardly be a better description of the aims and limitations of a school which, having failed to produce any artists with real temperament, tried to substitute theory for inspiration. Not even Menzel gave his etchings the accent he gave his wood-cuts *(Family by Lamplight).* Wilhelm Leibl (1844-1900) was almost the only German artist of the time who, particularly in his portraits, achieved some real strength and feeling.

In Italy, the great examples of Piranesi and Canaletto seemed to have been forgotten. Calamatta, the interpreter of Ingres, was followed by a myriad other reproductive engravers of the second rank and, with the exception of the graceful etchings of de Nittis, there appeared not to be a single engraver capable of producing anything but hasty and superficial work.

HONORÉ DAUMIER. *The Ass and the Two Robbers.* *1862.* Lithograph

Not content with having founded the Société des Aquafortistes, Cadart also arranged to send three stones to each of several artists: Bracquemond, Manet, Ribot, Legros and Fantin-Latour. Hédiart tells us that the set was designed to be issued as a collection. Manet produced *The Balloon,* Ribot *Reading Aloud,* Legros *Quarrymen at Montrouge* and Bracquemond *Horsemen.* Fantin-Latour, who had never touched a lithographic crayon in his life, was the most enthusiastic and used all three stones. When these came back to Lemercier, there was only one opinion: 'Horrible. Extravagant and crude. We can't possibly print them.' It is likely that the other lithographs got no better reception than the *Women at Embroidery.* Very few copies were printed and Cadart had to give up the idea of issuing them as a collection, thus retarding the revival of the lithograph by more than ten years.

As though exhausted by its too early flowering, lithography had long ceased to be regarded by either artists or publishers as anything except a cheap means of reproduction. Delacroix had left the lithographing of his works to Mouilleron and Le Roux, and Bertaut had abandoned publication of *Artistes contemporains* with its lithographs by Doré, Nanteuil, François and Baron. Printers used it only for the title pages of novels. 'All that remains,' wrote Burty, 'is to bury the last crayon-holder under the last stone and carve above it the motto of the vanquished patriot: Finis lithographiae.'

In his report on the 1878 exhibition, Delaborde commented that lithography, as then understood and practised, had lost all the spontaneity that used to be its main charm. It had sunk to a mere method of reproduction and so practically speaking lost its *raison d'être.* The contempt of art patrons for original lithography indeed equalled, if it did not surpass, the indifference with which they regarded etching. And yet this was at a time when Daumier was producing masterpiece after masterpiece for weekly publication in *Le Charivari.*

DAUMIER'S LATER LITHOGRAPHS

Daumier has often been accused of reacting to the boredom of the daily round, the restrictions imposed on him by the censorship and the ungrateful task of finding subjects among the commonplace vagaries of a bourgeois society, by neglecting his art. Under the Second Empire, say these critics, his engraving progressively declined and he took to repeating his earlier effects. These criticisms are due to the fact that, until Loys Delteil issued the final volumes of his illustrated Catalogue, Daumier's work during this period was very little known. After *Recollections of Artists, Le Charivari* gave up printing his lithographs 'on white' as it had done for *Men of the Law, Worthy Citizens, Robert Macaire, Ancient*

History, What more could one want? The Bathers, The Blue-stockings and his other admirable, widely reproduced sets of prints. Besides, even his most fanatical admirers balked at leafing through the voluminous tomes of *Charivari's* later issues. Bad ink, bad paper, bad printing and the substitution of photozincography for the use of stone, all combine to distort Daumier's superb black and white tones, that can only be seen now in one or two very rare proofs pulled before printing.

Disappointed alike by his public and his publishers, Daumier nevertheless still kept his integrity. There must have been moments when his inspiration failed; towards 1865, for example, when he reverted for a time in his contributions to the *Journal Amusant* or the *Journal pour rire,* to the minute bodies topped by enormous heads of his earlier period. But, apart from these, his draughtsmanship, far from falling off, was gaining progressively in power. The obscurity in which he now lived left him more time for painting, and many of the lithographs he was producing at this time almost simultaneously with his paintings contain more colour then ever. His drawing regained its earlier epic quality. As he could no longer criticize internal policy he devoted a long series of plates to European questions. He began again to substitute, for figures of individuals, great symbolic figures such as those in his *The Last Council of the Ex-Ministers* or *Parricide*. There was no other artist of his century who approached him in his gift for allegory. Despite Daumier's rough handling of the ancients, Baudelaire was right when he said that no one had a greater sense of the grandeur of classical times. The mantle in which he had draped the burlesque actors of his *Tragi-classical Character Studies* he now allowed to fall in gentle, moving folds round his figures of *France* or *Peace*. He depicts the struggles of powerful, statuesque figures, seemingly drawn with one movement of the crayon, and half naked beneath their covering veils. It was not only its costumes, but its gods that he borrowed from antiquity. *Death* is accompanied by *Time* with his sickle; *Mars* gestures beside them. *Europe* maintains herself precariously on a smoking cannon-ball; the *Future* appears in wrestler's shorts, eyes covered with a bandage, while below on the ground lie a scythe and an hour-glass. In *The Savings Bank* the nations are shown each piling up their stores of bullets. The *Statues of the future?* are Polycarpe, Bombardard, Eustache Fusillard, Barnabé Mitraillard. *Progress* is a horse, its eyes bound, turning round in a circle. '*Not shortened too much?*' Freedom is depicted as asking the Constitution which is trying on a dress. The year 1869 is drawn as Sisyphus, striving to roll a huge budget uphill. After war had broken out, *Death* supported by Bismarck points to a plain heaped with corpses. *Is the Empire at peace?* is a mass of smoking ruins; the *Square Napoléon* is paved with tombstones. A picture of a cannon surrounded by ruins is entitled *Landscape, 1870*. After the fall of the Empire, the eagle lies crushed beneath *Retribution*.

For the third time in his life, Daumier turned to political satire, although the suppression of *Le Charivari* made it impossible for him to take part in the struggle between the Versaillais and the Communards. France he depicts as a tree whose trunk has been blasted by lightning with, underneath, the legend, which may

CAMILLE COROT. *The Church Tower of Saint-Nicolas-lès-Arras. c. 1870.* Lithograph

EDOUARD MANET. *The Races*. Lithograph

well this time be his own, *Luckily the roots are deep*. *Peace (an Idyll)* shows Death in a little straw hat, sitting on a rock playing a trumpet. In *Risen at last* France, supported by the Loan, is rising to her feet watched in stupefaction by the world. One of the last of these lithographs is worthy to stand beside any he published under Louis-Philippe. Entitled *The Witnesses*, it shows a company of skeletons, some without heads, some dragging children behind them, some again pointing to the *Conseil de Guerre*, advancing on the court where Bazaine is being tried, demanding vengeance.

Whether or not Daumier wrote the legends for these cartoons himself, he illustrated them with a verve in no way inferior to that of his earlier period.

Even apart from their subject and legends, these lithographs, despite the bad printing, have an incomparable richness, and their tones are as generous as the feeling behind them. Daumier's imagination had grown with his philosophy,

ODILON REDON. *Beatrice*. *1897*. Colour lithograph

but without diminishing in any way the fundamental good sense shown in all his work, which invariably conveys a feeling of intimacy and unshakable sincerity together with a good humour compounded of strength, experience and the power of endurance. It is in the four thousand plates published in *La Caricature* and *Le Charivari* that the true soul of 19th-century France is to be found.

MANET, COROT, DEGAS, FANTIN-LATOUR

It was Burty who said that if the art of engraving were to die it would be for lack of a public, not for lack of artists. While lithography had apparently been abandoned and was to all intents and purposes officially dead, quite a number of artists were still experimenting with it individually.

Although Manet's lithographs are far less numerous than his etchings, they all bear the mark of the same sensitive talent. Not enough has been made of Daumier's influence on him in this field. It is less apparent in *The Balloon,* his first lithograph, but it can be seen clearly in *The Barricade* and *Civil War* (1871). There may, in a sense, be no real parallel between the tragedy of the room in the *Rue Transnonain* and Manet's dead rebel lying with his eyes staring upwards, but the resemblance between the two pictures is striking though it derives less from the subject than from the technique. The design of *Civil War,* the masterly handling of the composition and the sureness of touch are all admirable. In *The Races,* the three front horses are galloping towards us, all out, and their movement seems to have communicated itself to the whole picture so that stands, rails and sky seem to be carried along with them. The figures are hardly to be distinguished; they are no longer individuals but blotches of shadow. There can hardly be another engraving in which movement is carried to such a pitch of intensity.

Manet's contribution to engraved portraiture was equally important. His two portraits of Berthe Morisot, the one in outline only, the other with the light falling on her face which is framed in her hair, are drawn in the same incisive style and already hint at the 'sketchy' technique that was to be both used and abused by the artists of the next century. The influence the Japanese had on Manet's work is evident both in the lithographed illustrations he did for Edgar Allan Poe's *The Raven,* where aquatint successfully reproduces Poe's own sombre tones, and in a series of fluid etched landscapes of great charm that he did for Cros' *Fleuve* (1874) and which at the time represented something of a revolution. His *Punchinello,* which belongs to the same year, is significant less for itself than because it marks the beginnings of a new interest in colour lithography which, however, was not firmly established until over twenty years later, with Toulouse-Lautrec and other clients of the Clot printing works.

It was in 1871, at Arras and Douai, that Corot designed his set of twelve *autographies*. Like his etchings, their charm lies in the general composition, the relation of the figures to the plants and trees surrounding and dominating them,

CAMILLE COROT. *Horseman in a Wood.* *c. 1870.* Glass print

the simplicity with which Nature's familiar sights are evoked and the distinction spontaneously conferred on everyday objects. This combination of distinction and simplicity recalls some of Lamartine's tenderest passages but, with Corot, the feeling is even more serene and restrained. The willows, birches, poplars, oaks, are outlined against the sky, seeming to sway gently in the wind while their almost imperceptible movements are merged with the quivering light and echoed by those of the humble inhabitants of the place—peasants on horseback or gathering wood, men reading, family groups *(The Meeting, Horseman in the Reeds, The Gust of Wind, Philosophers' Repose)*.

In some plates, an Italian landscape is recalled by a hill-top crowned with a ruined temple; in others, a church tower or a cottage can be glimpsed through the branches. No theme could be simpler or more impressive than that of *Windmill at Quincy,* with its great fallen tree lying right across the foreground from bank to bank like a bridge. The density of leaves is sometimes suggested by plain hatchings looking as though drawn by pen or charcoal, but more often the whole plate has a miraculously soft grey tone as though made of silver dust. There is perhaps no other example of stone producing such delicate and tender effects. Corot had the unique gift of breathing individual life and character into everything he drew, however tenuous and unsubstantial in itself. Here or there his crayon stresses a little patch of shadow in a fold of the ground, in the dress of a passer-by; here or there a birch tree, a tower or a piece of sky is lighted up with a touch of pure white. With the genius of an angel, Corot also possessed a purely masculine vigour thanks to which his lithographs lost nothing through the transfer-paper, the use of which in any other hands could not have failed to soften their lines. In fact, it may actually have contributed towards preserving the subdued tones of the whole.

Corot's lithographs were done partly from memory, partly from sketches; he was fond of saying that he kept a copy of all his works in his eyes and in his heart. He never used the scraper or added further tint; the whole concept was complete before ever the work reached the printer. But though he thus worked in isolation, he had an instinctive knowledge of all the resources offered by the lithographic process. It is curious that he never seems to have discussed his lithographs with Daumier, one of his greatest friends.

His glass prints have points of comparison with both his etchings and his lithographs, this process, also used by Delacroix, Millet, Rousseau and Daubigny, being the bastard child of the other two. These prints, mostly on stiff paper, have preserved all their original freshness, while some have already acquired the bronzed patina of much earlier works. His two prints both entitled *Horseman in a Wood,* the *Souvenir of Ostia* and the *Gardens of Horace* are as beautiful as the best of the *autographies.* The incisions—if that is the right word for lines drawn with such delicate strength on the ink or collodion ground—seem to sparkle, while the light adds a thousand magic reflections as it irradiates the glass as through a prism.

Degas turned to lithography about 1875. While *Cirque Médrano, Café-Concert* and *Mme Bécar* may be said to have pointed the way to Toulouse-Lautrec, it is

EDGAR DEGAS. *The Bath.* *c. 1890.* Lithograph

THÉODORE FANTIN-LATOUR. *Roses.* *1879.* Lithograph

THÉODORE FANTIN-LATOUR. *Women at Embroidery*. Lithograph

probable also that Forain would never have discovered his true talent had it not been for Degas and his *Nude at the Bedroom Door, In the Wings,* or *Standing Nude.* His influence on Forain is apparent not only in the latter's choice of subject but also in his drawing.

For his lithographs, Degas seems to have done fewer states than for his etchings and certain of them, like *The Stage Box, Dog Song* or *In the Wings,* appear even to have been done direct. On the other hand, while the manner of *After the Bath* and *Standing Nude* is more abrupt and the indication of the contours even more summary, and while the meticulous technique of his earlier work has disappeared, the number of erasings, and use made of scraper and roulette show Degas to have been under the same compulsion as led him, in his old age, to make alterations to certain of his paintings and pastels. In *After the Bath* this alteration has been carried so far as to make the last state of the picture hardly recognisable.

As will be seen later, Pissarro also contributed a set of twelve scenes of everyday life to the list of masterpieces produced in the same medium. But the most important of all the artists whom his example caused to experiment with lithography was undoubtedly Fantin-Latour.

ODILON REDON. *Captive Pegasus.* *1889.* Lithograph

Fantin-Latour's art is essentially one of transposition.   Therein lie at once its charm and its limitations.   Even the compositions taken direct from life and owing nothing to fancy or caprice still have something theatrical or out-of-date about them.   In many cases his lithographs were inspired by his paintings; both the admirable *Roses* (1879) and *Eve* are translations of his own canvases.   It is a method that is apt to dilute inspiration, and to this defect must be added the further weakening due to the use of transfers.   We know from Hédiart that when he received the proofs, Fantin-Latour hardly took the trouble to give them the minimum of touching up before printing.   This is one of the great difficulties confronting lithographers.   While the use of transfers saves the artist the trouble of manipulating inconvenient pieces of stone, it has the disadvantage of sometimes making him forget what he is losing by no longer working on the stone direct.   If so, then lithography ceases to be a technique in its own right and becomes merely a useful but uninteresting method of reproduction.   The use of transfer-paper is only allowable in order to plan the composition.   Thereafter, the picture must be completed by aquatint or crayon, and by further shading or scraping direct on to the stone.   One artist fully aware of this was Redon. After he had once learnt the use of the transfer-paper from Fantin-Latour, he always afterwards worked closely with his printer, a method that put him, technically speaking, far ahead not only of Fantin-Latour but of other artists, such as Renoir or Forain, who were too apt to rely on the transfers alone.

Fantin-Latour's own idealism and culture and the understanding with which he tried to reconcile the world of reality with that of imagination gave his work a singular charm.   Where it falls short is in vigour.   For all his spiritual kinship with Lamartine, the weakness apparent in his work is nowhere counterbalanced by the pithiness of expression characteristic of the author of the *Méditations*.   There is always something hesitant in it; the world it represents is an unreal, nebulous world, peopled with sexless figures suspended between earth and heaven.   Fantin-Latour had taste, delicacy, and a gift for composition; but he lacked a sense of movement.   In spite of having been Lecoq de Boisbaudran's favourite pupil, he had none of the visual clarity that made the strength of a Daumier or a Degas. He worked from memory but it was a pallid memory.   Hence his most successful engravings are apt to be those in which he is concentrating on reproducing faithfully, in the still light of an interior, a bunch of flowers, a self-portrait or a portrait head of one of his sisters at her reading or sewing.   In these, there is real feeling to back up the strength of the drawing.

Champfleury nicknamed Fantin-Latour the 'Schumannist' and many of his lithographs take their titles from the symphonic poems of Berlioz, Brahms, Schumann or Wagner.   They carry a muted, somewhat sad echo of past Venetian splendours.   His Eves and Venuses seem to belong to Titian, Veronese or Giorgione, and there is no disputing the quality of a talent that could express so much charm in black and white.   To study these engravings, of which we possess over a hundred and fifty, is to realise what Seurat might have produced had he turned to lithography.   Both artists had the same gift for producing dazzling highlights and for making white stand out brilliantly against black.   But in

ODILON REDON. *Origins.* Lithograph

Seurat, as in Redon, there is a sense of mystery that makes the most ordinary form and the least legendary figure look as if it belonged to a higher plane. It does not matter that, urged on by his own inventive powers or the infectious example of the master whose work he is translating, Fantin-Latour sometimes bursts apart the narrow framework of his own dream. With his momentary reminiscences of Prud'hon and the 18th century, he was the one artist, with the possible exception of Daumier, who knew how to bring allegory to life and give some appearance of reality to those great, shining figures that are represented as bestowing palms and crowns on famous painters, musicians or poets, or carving their names on marble plaques.

ODILON REDON. *Dreams.* Lithograph

THE LITHOGRAPHS OF ODILON REDON

Redon's early etchings, done before 1870, are in the direct line of descent from Bresdin. But his first set, dated 1879 and entitled *Dreams,* is stamped with all his own individuality. Thereafter, until 1900, he continued to produce, alongside his paintings, a constant flow of prints which showed him to be one of France's greatest imaginative artists since Delacroix. No doubt he would not have produced what he did had he never seen the ceiling of the *Galerie d'Apollon* or the *Jacob Struggling with the Angel,* but the feeling stirred in us by *Captive Pegasus, Nudes surprised by Centaurs,* the *Reader, Closed Eyes* or the wonderful series of

Dreams and the *Temptations of St Anthony* is nevertheless entirely different from that provoked by the work of Delacroix. With Redon, we are at once transported into the unknown world of things unexplained and unexplored, whose proportions might be those of another planet.

True, we are struck and perhaps irritated by the strangeness of some of his compositions and their macabre or grotesque fantasies, full of moving eyes, spectres with human heads, and grimacing monsters. But in his other work Redon subdued his feverish imagination to his real aim, which was to 'transcend the object', free himself from the slavery of the real, shoot his arrow over the roof. 'The Impressionists are too low-ceilinged to please me,' he used to say. At these moments, we can admire him unreservedly, as we admire his predecessors, Dürer, Bosch, Bruegel, Leonardo, Callot, Tintoretto, Goya, Delacroix or Bresdin, in whose imaginings there was nothing childish or absurd, and who opened new horizons to the art of painting.

Redon always observes what Remy de Gourmont called 'the logic of imagination.' He never offends our reason. He may distort but in doing so he never loses touch with truth. He refused to be bound by the traditional rules of perspective and subordinated everything in a picture to the light composition which he regarded as infinitely more important than either literary background or actual presentation. His skill in combining contrasting values and in indicating light and heat was extraordinary. Sometimes, there is a violent and dramatic contrast of black and white; sometimes, the whole picture seems permeated with shadow or luminosity. His whites emerge gradually from the shadows or flash out as though caught in sunlight; his greys are of an infinite variety; his blacks are sometimes dark as the Pit, sometimes rich and sensuous as purple velvet. Perhaps Seurat is the only other artist to have achieved blacks so splendid. These lithographs are masterpieces, apart altogether from their subject. They delight the eye even before they captivate the mind. None of them, except one or two like *Beatrice* or *The Shulamite Woman*, are coloured and yet colour is everywhere suggested.

His general contours once established with the help of the transfer-paper, Redon worked and worked over the stone, like Delacroix over *Macbeth consulting the Witches,* in which all the light values were added by the scraper. In order to obtain the brilliant whites needed to contrast with the deep blacks obtained by aquatint, Redon used glass paper, sometimes boring so deeply into the stone that, once the printing had been done, it had to be ground down several millimetres. These unaccustomed methods caused considerable dismay among the professionals. Redon has left an account of his sessions in the printing works and his contacts with his assistants, some of whom, like Belfond at Lemercier's and Clot, were first-class craftsmen. 'I believe', he wrote, 'that I have given my imagination free rein in demanding from lithography everything it has to give. Each of my plates is the result of a passionate search for the utmost that can be extracted from the combined use of crayon, paper and stone.'

In some of his other work he used neither aquatint nor scraper but concentrated on contours, ignoring the intricacies of light and shade. This is the method

FÉLICIEN ROPS. *The Lace-maker*. *1876*. Soft ground etching and dry point

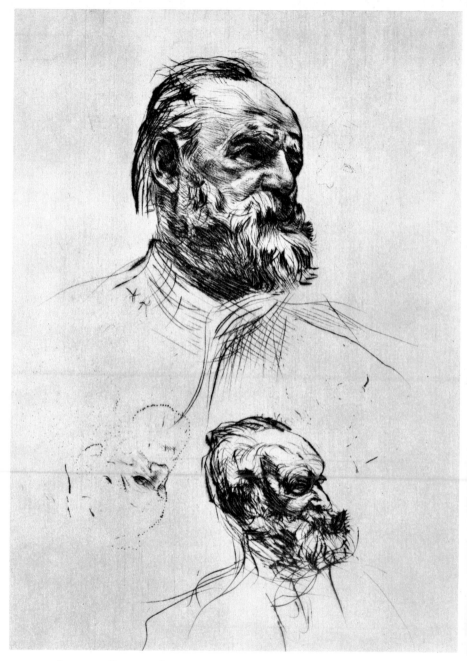

AUGUSTE RODIN. *Portrait of Victor Hugo.* *c. 1885.* Dry point

used in the portraits he produced at intervals from 1900 to 1908, the last lithographs he did.   These likenesses of Sérusier, Vuillard, and other of his friends, are done with the minute care of a crayon by Holbein or Clouet and in them it is the real that predominates. The characteristic lines of each face are drawn with fine, close strokes of the greasy crayon.   There is no searching after effect, no facile emotion in the depicting of a particular smile or expression.   At once natural and slightly idealised, they are true likenesses and achieve a depth that none of his contemporaries approached, except perhaps Degas, Toulouse-Lautrec or Carrière and they by totally different methods.   These portraits alone should give cause for reflection to those who regard Redon as a writer *manqué,* whereas he never ceased, with the clear-sightedness that characterised everything he wrote, 'to seek in nature a leavening element...to give an illusion of life to creatures essentially unreal...to harness the logic of the visible to the service of the invisible.'

ISOLATION OF THE PAINTER-ENGRAVERS
BETWEEN 1875 AND 1900

After having considered the work of various masters up to the end of the last century it is now time to turn back and examine, alongside the outstanding figures whose work was for long known only to a few, a band of artists whose success with the general public was considerably greater.

We have seen how Cadart continued his work beyond 1880 with his *Illustration Nouvelle* and *Eau-forte moderne.   La Gazette des Beaux-Arts* and *Art* also provided an outlet for a number of engravers, while the *Artiste,* which had at one time been an excellent paper, was shortly to publish Rodin's portrait of Victor Hugo as its swan-song.   Collectors and dealers continued, however, to concentrate on reproductive engraving.   Cadart's Catalogue of 1878 gives the following prices: artist's proof of Manet's *Gipsies,* 6 francs; artist's proof of a set of ten etchings by Jongkind, 60 francs; a portfolio of six etchings by Delacroix, 30 francs; artist's proof of a Meryon or a Seymour Haden sold for 15 francs.   This state of affairs lasted until almost the end of the century, certainly until the founding of the *Société des peintres-graveurs français* in 1889.   The lack of interest taken in original engraving is apparent from the records of any of the societies responsible for protecting the interests of professional artists.   Neither the *Société des Lithographes français,* nor that of the *Aquafortistes français,* nor that of the *Graveurs au burin* showed more critical acumen than did the international exhibitions arranged by *Noir et Blanc.*   The *Rétrospective de la Gravure,* published in 1892, is hopelessly incomplete and mentions neither Géricault, Delacroix nor Manet. The only exhibitions worthy of note that provided a link between past and present were *La Lithographie* arranged in 1890 by Jean Gigoux and Français, and the *Centenaire de la lithographie* held in 1895.

Reproductive etching was, indeed, at that time tending to supplant line engraving, and etchers like Gaucherel, Jacquemart, Chauvel, Waltner and Focillon were devoting much care and attention to translating the work of others. At the same time, Lalauze, Champollion and Le Rat were engaged in producing small illustrations and vignettes for books. The public was strongly attracted to Meissonier's work, and it was not long before etching began to suffer from the same elaborate detail and frigid style as the old line engraving. Good work was being ousted by finicky, monotonous engraving, devoid of any artistic thought or inspiration. From this dreary background emerges the figure of Félicien Rops.

For thirty years, Rops was destined to eclipse all his fellow artists. The most insignificant book was sure of a sale if it included one of his frontispieces, and he was as popular with the intelligentsia as with the public at large. In his earliest lithographs, published in *Le Charivari,* everything—types, composition, design—appears to have been borrowed from either Daumier or Gavarni. His etchings show no greater originality; their drawing is uncertain and they contain nothing clear-cut. The term soft ground seems to take on a new justification. In his water-colours, his ingenuity suggested the adoption of methods of illumination and other complicated procedures, and there was equally no engraving process that he did not try. Throughout his work, true imagination is always sacrificed to literary or theatrical effect, true technical skill to virtuosity. Rops was one of the first to use photogravure for his backgrounds, and thus set a dangerous example. The originality of a print is bound to be compromised from the start if the first stage in its production is a mechanical one.

Various great minds, ambitious to encourage the transposition of art forms in the name of Naturalism or Symbolism, and spurred on by the poetic equivalents they supposed themselves to have discovered in *The Absinthe-drinker, Messalina, The Dance of Death,* or *Mors syphilitica,* thought they had found, in this gipsy, a brother to Baudelaire or Edgar Allen Poe. The eroticism of *Theft and Prostitution ruling the world,* the *Old Faun* or the *Lady with a Pig* strikes us today as merely childish, while nothing could be more pedestrian than Rops' vignettes, despite the winged Cupids with which he has scattered them. In contrast, Morin or Willette, carrying on the charming tradition of the decorative artists of the 18th century, show a real gift of imagination. The beauty of their emblematic devices is equalled by the variety of their themes and their ingenuity in the use of type. Whatever the admiration felt by Rops for the Parisian woman, 'that incredible compound of cardboard, nerves and face-powder' (the description is his own), his attitude towards her always hovered between that of a dazzled undergraduate and that of a provincial up in town on a spree.

It may be left to Ramiro to describe these drawings which were done from imagination and lack either strength or correct technique, as possessing 'the

PAUL-CÉSAR HELLEU. *Portrait of James McNeill Whistler.* *1897.* Dry point

integrity of an Ingres'. If the name of Rops deserves to survive at all, it is for one or two crowded plates smacking of the real countryside *(Old Catherine, Flemish Folly, The Old Graver)*. Of all his work, it is these that show the most careful observation and the most real feeling. The rest are too reminiscent of those depressing collections of old ribbons and intimate toilet articles that one comes across when clearing out a dead woman's drawers.

Another reputation hardly less surprising than that gained by Rops is that of James Tissot. He however had some feeling for movement and elegance, which gave his works the sad position of owing their popularity to a transient fashion with which they disappeared. But Tissot's work will come into its own again for its value to the social historian. This has already happened with Paul Helleu's dry points which, after attracting great popularity, had fallen into an undeserved disrepute.

FÉLIX BUHOT.   *The Four-wheelers.   1876.*   Etching

MARY CASSATT. *Feeding the Ducks. 1895.* Coloured etching

Desboutins called etching 'the horror inside the plaster', in allusion to the hazards of biting. It might be possible to agree with him, had not his own work degenerated into a facile artificiality due to the endless commissioned pictures he was obliged to produce and which ended by quenching his original inspiration. His most successful works are the dry points he did at a single sitting, in which his zest and good humour enabled him, without too much difficulty, to produce a series of lively portraits of many of the best artists and writers of his time. He also did a little set of self-portraits under such titles as *Man with a Pipe, Man with a Palette* and *Man in a Large Hat* which show a greater economy of line than most of his other work.

For a long time, Rops, Tissot, Desboutins, Helleu and numberless other small illustrators passed for the masters of engraving of the late 19th century, which remained resolutely hostile to originality and indifferent to the treasures hidden away in the portfolios of Degas, Pissarro, Rodin and Carrière.

It is difficult to know exactly what place to assign to Buhot (1847-1898). A romantic at heart, but living in a period when the cult of realism was at its height, his early work consisted of small harbour scenes of much charm often showing considerable imaginative gifts. But he soon abandoned picturesque, anecdotal subjects for the masterpieces of engraving that resulted from his journeys to England (the two *Westminsters* and the *Disembarking*) or Valognes, and for a series of views of Paris *(Taverne du Bagne, Place Pigalle, etc.)*. While Daubigny loved the morning, Buhot preferred heavy, misty skies, and his most successful plates are those showing the dramatic effects of dusk on towns or coasts. No one approaches his gift for reproducing the atmosphere of a London or Paris evening, the reflections in the wet pavements, the passers-by hurrying along and looking, with their umbrellas, like strange birds flying between heaven and earth. He saw his great capitals with a very different eye from Meryon, Whistler or Jongkind.

In its complexity, his technique can be compared only to that of Degas. He used every known process, varied the inking, selected papers of differing quality, and touched up his proofs by hand. For this skilful and delicate technique he invented the charming name of 'a little chamber symphony'. His plates are surrounded by *Remarques*, variations on his central theme which he christened *'marges symphoniques'*. His *Small Pond, Thatched Cottages* and *Sheepfolds* are examples of familiar scenes treated in a lofty style. In his great symbolic pictures, like *Genius of Dead Towns* or *Château des hiboux,* his lyric quality is apparent, as also in some of his drawings or etchings which are the kind of thing a Victor Hugo might have produced, had he adopted copper not the pen as his medium.

Buhot's life was, as he called it himself, a succession of 'épreuves', playing on the word in its dual sense of trial and printer's proof, and towards its conclusion he sank into a kind of gloomy mysticism, as black as his own inks. *'Les épreuves'*, he once wrote, *'m'ont mangé tout entier, temps et cervelle.'* He was a curious figure, like all those for whom engraving is not just a profession, but a consuming passion.

Albert Besnard first took up etching during his stay in London between 1879 and 1883, during which he got to know Legros. *The End of it All* impresses not only by its undoubted depth of feeling, but even more by its magnificent composition and luminosity. 'Rome,' they say, 'made Besnard,' but should they not rather have said Venice? Certainly, the *Portrait of Madame Besnard* and *The Silk Dress* (1877) both have a truly Venetian opulence. Besnard's etchings present a symphony of light values, achieved by his favourite back-to-the-light effects, and a combination of strongly incised lines and others more lightly etched-in with additions in dry point that give a silk-like sheen to the harder blacks produced by the biting. His work shows exceptional vigour and facility, besides a natural distinction. However unequal some of it may be, prints such as *In the Ashes, The Sick Mother* or *Reading by Lamplight* reveal undeniable qualities of brilliance and grace which are emphasised by the clear-cut biting. His inspiration is akin to the achievements of the Impressionists, and he knows how to

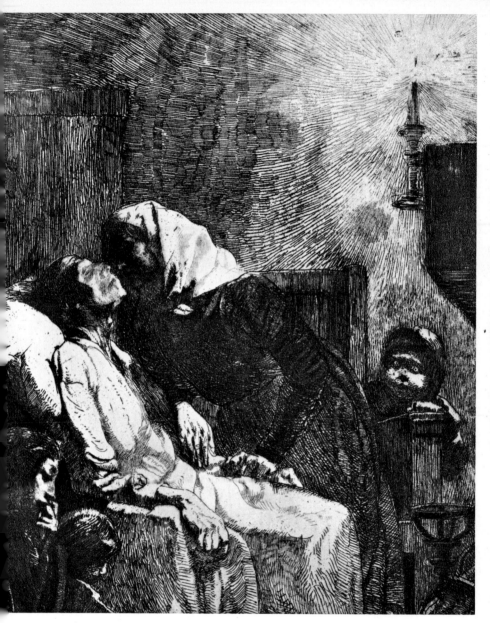

PAUL ALBERT BESNARD. *The End of it All.* *c. 1880.* Etching

convey a sense of the open air *(Bathing at Talloires, Horse-market in Algiers).* Many of his plates are slashed across with great hatchings like those of Degas, while the brilliance of his portraits makes him a forerunner of Zorn. A virtuoso who was sometimes carried away by the desire for effect, he nevertheless found in etching the medium best suited to his gifts.

One sign of a born engraver is that the mere contact with his copper, wood or stone can prove a source of immediate and unlooked-for inspiration. Many a good but undistinguished artist has found, on turning to engraving, that he can produce work of a quality of which neither his temperament nor his understanding had hitherto given promise. Such was Anders Zorn who may, perhaps, be

Anders Léonard Zorn. *Portrait of Rosita Mauri. 1889.* Etching

allowed to count among the French engravers as it was in France that he had his earliest successes. It was not until 1884 that Zorn achieved anything like an individual style. He indicates his forms by little, parallel lines of an astonishing quickness and vivacity, almost reminding one at times of a wilder Manet. The light is caught between the strokes, and the movement of the planes suggested in the manner of a sculptor. With dazzlingly swift strokes, Zorn seizes, as it were, the faces of fifty people. His electric style has a brusque charm that compels admiration.

At a time when Impressionism was just coming into fashion, it is easy to understand the enthusiasm provoked by Zorn's *Portrait of Rosita Mauri* in which he uses the same swift lines that barely distinguish between form and shadow and scratch the plate as a match strikes the edge of the box, but from which emerges a charming face. But, whatever the brilliance of the *Portrait of Ernest Renan, The Cigarette, The Waltz* or that near-masterpiece for boldness of movement and expression, *The Toast*, art of this type must in the long run confess to limitations and, despite his gift of speed, Zorn never approaches artists like Legros or Rodin in depth. There is often a certain triviality about his nudes. Even when depicting a woman from the fashionable world of London or Paris, he keeps his peasant directness. The sensuality and vigour that no anxiety can alter are not without their charm, but his likenesses of *Verlaine* or *Renan*, for example, are no more than skin deep. His lightening shafts are never accompanied by the thunder of the great authors; he never knows the dizziness of gazing into the depths of the mind behind the face. He is aiming at a summary, not a synthesis, and grief is a closed book to him. Zorn has been compared to Rembrandt but his real kinship is with Van Dyck.

PAUL ALBERT BESNARD. *The Sick Mother.* *1889.* Etching

Auguste Rodin. *Cupids guiding the World. c. 1881.* Dry point

RODIN'S DRY POINTS

Although they number only eleven in all, Rodin's engravings constitute the most important body of engraved work ever produced by a sculptor. His first plate dates from 1881, when he was living in London with Legros, and his *Cupids guiding the World* actually dance across the back of a plate engraved by the latter. *Spring* and *La Ronde* belong to 1883. Roger-Marx—the first to catalogue Rodin's dry points and call attention to their importance—says of his portraits of *Victor Hugo, Becque* and *Antonin Proust,* done between 1884 and 1886, that in them 'he achieved the full expression of his ideal. He used his steel point almost as though it were a graver or grater, treating the copper as roughly as though it had been marble. He attacks it with a violence that dies away into a series of light, closely-

AUGUSTE RODIN. *Portrait of Monsieur Bugne. c. 1885.* Dry point

woven cross-hatchings, succeeding the heavy strokes of his original outline. His lines follow the modelling of his subject and never miss the faintest inflection. The lines and contrasts gradually build up into a picture in which the artist's struggle with his material can clearly be seen and which allows the characteristics of the model's face gradually to emerge. These portraits are unique, for their life and for the extraordinary variety of relief they show.

Rodin's portraits are at least as powerful as any by Dürer, Rembrandt, Ingres or Goya. Beside them, even the portraits of Manet and Degas have a petrified look, while those of Zorn or Besnard cease to be remarkable except for their restlessness. In his full-face portrait of *Victor Hugo,* by some prescience the poet's face is shown as the meeting-place of night and day; the eyes are depths encompassing the whole world, but despite this, there is no sense of over-emphasis. The attitude is conventional; we are looking at some little notary on whom the mantle of genius has suddenly descended.

To the same period as *La Ronde* and *Spring* belong the Indian ink and gouache drawings inspired by Dante's *Inferno*, which have a dynamic power equal to the drawings of Michelangelo, Rembrandt or Daumier.

PISSARRO, SISLEY, MARY CASSATT, BERTHE MORISOT

Of all the engravings produced by the Impressionists, taking the term in its widest sense, those of Pissarro and Degas stand out both for number and quality. Monet always refused to touch either point or greasy crayon and Cézanne, Renoir, Gauguin, Sisley and Guillaumin only produced an occasional lithograph or etching. Pissarro, however, with characteristic tenacity and the open and flexible mind that enabled him to assimilate such a wide variety of influences, made himself master of a complex technique that was constantly enriched by his own work.

If he said little about his etching, it was probably due to the poor opinion of engraving held by his friends; but until the end of his life it continued to be a

CAMILLE PISSARRO. *Place du Havre (Paris)*. Lithograph

CAMILLE PISSARRO. *Self-portrait. 1890.* Etching

passion with him. He attached so much importance to this side of his work that he kept a complete record of the numbers of printings, in his notebooks as well as on the impressions. For a single etching, we have nine, ten, up to sixteen states. Nor are these 'states' in the somewhat over-simplified sense sometimes given to the term by collectors; they are successive versions of a picture, in which not only its general aspect, lighting or atmosphere may differ, but the composition as a whole. Highly critical of his own work, Pissarro tried always, once the subject was no longer before his eyes, to escape from the immediate sensation it had aroused in him and distill the essence of his underlying emotion. These series of states enable us to see him escaping from reality in order the better to express it; new figures are introduced, earlier ones eliminated, a fore-

MARY CASSATT. *La Toilette.* *1891.* Colour print with dry point and aquatint

Mary Cassatt.   *The Letter.*   *1891.*   Colour print with dry point and aquatint

ALFRED SISLEY. *The Banks of the Loing. 1890.* Etching

ground is stressed, a background softened, an attitude corrected. Regardless of the season, he will cover a leafless tree with foliage, lighten a sky or darken it with clouds. In the same way, he treats the elements as if they belonged to him and alters the distribution of his shadows by introducing twilight or rainfall. It is fascinating to follow the successive stages of his work on a single plate and see it coming to life under our eyes and finding its unity through a thousand vicissitudes.

Pissarro's first etchings were strongly influenced by Corot and even more by Millet, but as early as 1874 he produced a portrait of *Cézanne* in pure etching of outstanding power. From 1879 onwards, he used aquatint to heighten the tones in his work, vary his values and obtain from the copper the same variety of greys that he achieved on his canvases. A thousand little dots, like fine rain, increase the contrasts and the transitions. Insufficient attention has hitherto been paid to the affinities between aquatint and the other divisionist processes whose discovery and use caused Pissarro considerable, although short-lived, alarm.

His usual method was to engrave the outline of his subject on the plate either by biting or with the dry point before laying the aquatint ground for which he, like Degas, used salt. Thereafter came the minute routine of burnishing, scraping, erasing, hatching and cross-hatching. Shadows and contours would be reinforced or softened and sometimes a second grain added, of a different texture from the first. Thus, in the *Girl Bathing and Geese,* we can follow and share the various doubts felt by the artist. While working on the tenth state (out of sixteen) he erased practically everything from the plate, hammered it, and restored the lightness and transparency of the earlier states.

Pissarro developed his themes in innumerable different ways. If he worked from the simple to the complex, he also did the opposite. He was well aware that the measure of true richness is the sacrifices it has entailed. *Landscapes at the Hermitage, Twilight, Woman emptying a Pail, Meadow and Mill at Osny, View of Pontoise, Osny Church, Potato Harvest, Château de Busagny, Girl tending Geese, Church and Farm at Eragny, Girl Bathing and Geese,* and *Haymakers at Eragny* can be considered true masterpieces, although even these could have been improved had not the artist often been compelled, for reasons of economy, to replace copper by zinc which, though it has a peculiar warmth, rapidly loses its receptivity.

Of the artists who exhibited their work with the Impressionists, apart from Degas and Pissarro, only Renoir, Sisley, Guillaumin, Mary Cassatt and Berthe Morisot produced any serious work on copper.

Sisley did no more than a set of four little landscapes entitled *The Banks of the Loing* (1890) though these are enough to show the delicacy and acute sensibility of his vision. Guillaumin produced a rather larger number of etchings which have the same rough brilliance as his paintings. Cézanne's engraved work consists of a small portrait, one nude and one landscape. Renoir's lithographs and etchings are all subsequent to 1890.

Mary Cassatt, on the contrary, knew Pissarro, Desboutins and Degas, and owed to her friendship with the latter her familiarity with a part of his work that he always kept most jealously to himself, and which was not properly known until after his death. Mary Cassatt began engraving before 1880 and the Catalogue of her work made by A.D. Breeskin contains nearly two hundred plates. From the beginning, she showed a masculine vigour and a contempt for facile charm that preserved her, whatever her subjects, from the weakness so often apparent in dry point work. Her subjects were always women and children, as though to compensate for the maternity she herself was denied. As a single woman, she had to imagine for herself her gestures of love and protection. There is a uniform air of happiness about these intimate scenes, and they lack the depth, due to personal experience, characteristic of Renoir, Carrière and Suzanne Valadon's portraits of their own children. All the same, her instinct remained sure and, where others too often lapsed into triviality or pathos, she always retained her dignity. She may sometimes make us smile, but the last word always belongs to her fundamental good sense and, above all, her exquisite drawing. 'It is intolerable that a woman should draw so well,' said Degas.

Her set of ten colour prints, of which only twenty-five copies were printed, appeared in 1891, and were so directly influenced by the coloured wood-cuts of Utamaro and Hokusai that she did not hesitate to entitle one of them 'Imitation

BERTHE MORISOT. *Self-portrait with Daughter.* *c. 1890.* Dry point

AUGUSTE LOUIS LEPÈRE.   *Paris under snow, view from the top of Saint-Gervais.*   *1890.*
Woodcut

of a Japanese engraving'.   Their colouring is admirably fresh and delicate and never conceals the vigour of the contours.

These, together with the sets done by Bonnard, Vuillard and Toulouse-Lautrec, are undoubtedly the most successful colour engravings we have.   But while *La Toilette, The Letter, The Coiffure* and *In the Bus* are certainly masterpieces of discreet concision, they cannot make us forget the sensitive distinction of light, uncrowded, monochrome prints like *Teatime, Mother and Child, The Sick Child* or *The Book,* that look as if they had been done at a single sitting.   Mary Cassatt always worked directly on to the plate from models who, in the nature of things, did not keep still long and this meant working quickly.   Her lines are swift and decisive.   The backgrounds, and even some of the figures, are summarised in large sweeping strokes, while the homely attitudes in the foreground—a mother's hand enclosing a pair of tiny feet, her lap at once cradle and throne are rendered with the utmost charm *(A Mother's Kiss, Bed-time, The Breast, La Toilette).* The term dry point describes not inaptly the remoteness and the dignity always preserved by Whistler's fellow-countrywoman, even in her most fashionable or most familiar scenes.

Berthe Morisot's eight little dry points produced between 1888 and 1890 *(The Drawing Lesson, Little Girl with a Cat)*, are not unlike those of Mary Cassatt in their subject and lightness of touch; but the feeling behind them is different. Corot's former pupil had a spontaneity and tenderness that were lacking in the cruder and stiffer work of the elder of the two artists. The life in Berthe Morisot's dry point is fresher and shows more animal spirits. They have nothing in common with Manet or Renoir, but there is something ingenuous and almost child-like in them that occasionally foreshadows Bonnard.

ORIGINAL ENGRAVING FROM 1889 TO 1900

FOUNDATION IN 1889 OF THE SOCIÉTÉ DES PEINTRES-GRAVEURS

The Société des Aquafortistes having failed in its attempt to win the general public over to etching, twenty years went by during which many good artists worked away in the background, producing engravings merely for their own pleasure. But about 1888 there began a movement to centralise efforts hitherto dispersed. It was headed by two men, both highly skilled in technique but equally aware that technique alone, unsupported by talent, is useless. These were Bracquemond, still full of faith and enthusiasm, and the charming and ingenious Henri Guérard.

It would be impossible to over-estimate the part played by their Society, whose motto might be 'Faithful and disinterested'. By its annual and retrospective exhibitions, it is still proving today that the present is never divorced from the past, since the same forces are constantly being reborn under new names.

The Peintres-Graveurs français can claim with pride that they have appreciated and adopted every great artist, without exception, who has appeared or reached maturity during the past seventy years. The list of their Presidents alone is enough: Bracquemond, Rodin, Eugène Carrière, Forain, Besnard, Lepère, Jacques Beltrand. Their Catalogues show that the moment any artist shows signs of true greatness he is invited to join their group. This is true generosity and farsightedness. Usually, an artistic coterie starts off with a flourish of trumpets and, despite the clash of temperaments, forms a single united body. Then the day comes when differences become more acute; without admitting it, the group resents the fact that it is getting older and in order to defend its privileges takes up an aggressive attitude towards the younger generation.

From the start, the *Peintres-Graveurs* assumed a leading role. They inspired new confidence in collectors and in the artists themselves, and filled the gaps left by the lack of enterprise of other societies and the mediocrity of the engraving shown in contemporary exhibitions. Interest re-awoke on all sides, and critics, publishers, printers and print-sellers began to work together, although without always succeeding in finding the necessary public support. Within a short time, spurred on by Lepère and Tony Beltrand, *L'Image* was conducting a campaign to bring back wood engraving. With the help of Marty, Roger-Marx founded *L'Estampe originale* among whose contributors were to be Rodin, Renoir, Gauguin, Toulouse-Lautrec and Redon, and later Bonnard, Vuillard and Roussel. The same names are to be found in the portfolios of Vollard's *Peintres-*

JEAN-FRANÇOIS RAFFAELLI. *Waste-ground.* Etching

graveurs, as well as in *L'Epreuve, Pan* and *Germinal.* The new wave of opinion created was such that not only did masters like Degas and Pissarro, who had abandoned engraving, now return to it, but wood engraving, etching and lithography began to attract more and more new artists. Some of these, like Renoir and Cézanne, belonged to the older generation; others, like Gauguin, Carrière, Toulouse-Lautrec, Maillol, Bonnard and Vuillard, belonged to the generations that followed the Impressionists. For the past half-century, illustrating had been confined largely to professional illustrators and had become correspondingly mediocre; but now book illustration was to be saved by concerted effort by painters, and the resulting publications were to include *Les Histoires naturelles, Daphnis et Chloé, Parallèlement, Le Jardin des Supplices* and *A Rebours,* although it was to take another thirty years before they would be fully appreciated.

There is something epic in this great united struggle to bring back the print in all its forms: black and white or coloured, posters or illustrations. There was a feeling of youth in the air and that youth, which was regarded as so revolutionary, was bringing back the best traditions of the past. It is impossible in a book of this size to enumerate all those who responded to the call of Guérard and Bracquemond or do more than indicate the strength of the movement. No other period has seen such a flowering, such high hopes or such numbers of engravers. Unhappily, the enthusiasm and hopefulness lasted barely twelve years before the indifference of the public once again smothered the spirit of originality. With one or two exceptions, from the beginning of the 20th century until the end of the first World War, engraving was relying entirely on its past momentum.

SOME VIRTUOSI: LE PÈRE, LEGRAND, HELLEU.
A LANDSCAPE SCHOOL

As we have seen, copper engraving was constantly being enriched by the work, much of it unknown at the time, of artists such as Degas, Pissarro or Mary Cassatt. But towards 1890 there was a marked renewal of interest in the use of wood and stone, although this did not diminish the interest in etching and dry point to which many artists, among them Auguste Lepère, Louis Legrand and Helleu, were devoting a considerable amount of their time. Without abandoning wood engraving to which, as we have seen, he devoted much time, wit and ingenuity, Lepère discovered in etching about 1889, 'a flexible medium that encourages experiment and is especially successful with drawing and effects of light and shade.' Taking Bracquemond, Paul Renouard, Delâtre—and Rembrandt— as his masters, Lepère experimented endlessly with his incising, biting and printing. After so many years spent meticulously transposing the work of others on to wood, magnifying glass in hand, now that he was his own master he felt free to alter the design itself as well as the light composition. He was still under the influence of Vierge and Morin, as well as of his own past as an

JULES CHÉRET. *Latin Quarter*. Colour lithograph

illustrator, and what attracted him was the picturesque. He looked for this everywhere, in new and old districts, along the banks of the Seine, in buses or in river steamers. He soon achieved a kind of mastery in his views of Paris *(The Apple Market, Bièvre et Saint-Séverin)*, as well as in his provincial scenes (Amiens, Beauvais, Rheims, Provins). But while in his work on wood he moved from the complex to the simple, aiming more and more at synthesis and the affirmation of contours, his etching shows a preoccupation with the enrichment and variation of his technique. Much of its charm results from the workmanlike care with which he regulates the depth of his incisions and biting. He tried also to make use of various methods of printing to strengthen some of his effects. But, sincere as his work is, and perhaps because his youth was spent either in reproducing or in illustrating the work of others, even his original compositions have the look of an interpretation. Brilliant and intelligent as he was, he never succeeded in creating on copper a masterpiece equal to those he achieved on wood. He had the manual skill and the mental alertness, but no real originality.

Impulsive and somewhat crude, Louis Legrand fell at one time under the influence of Félicien Rops' eroticism and satanism, but this was soon modified by the influence of Toulouse-Lautrec and Degas. His inspiration was sincere enough, but his work relies too much on external aids to be moving. Although he fell a victim to the passion for aquatint and experimented widely with the various types of grounds, he was not, contrary to what might be expected, in any sense a Primitive. But when he felt a sincere emotion he was able to reproduce it, whence the charm of one or two plates showing children *(Fleurs de lit)*. Like Helleu, Louis Legrand was a victim of his own facility, but he nevertheless gives us a picture of his time.

Paul Renouard found etching a convenient method of reporting what he saw. Rassenfosse, a virtuoso of soft-ground etching, can be described as an inferior Rops. John Lewis Brown, who specialised in military or sporting scenes, found colour lithography the best medium for his precise and elegant drawings.

Helleu gained his first successes with plates drawn with the diamond point, which cuts copper as a skate cuts ice, producing an effect as free and bold as a drawing. He was an admirer of Watteau and Lancret, and his dry points express all the fleeting elegance and natural coquetry of the contemporary Parisienne; he had the courage to love fashion at the risk of one day ceasing to be the fashion himself. He was more faithful to the spirit of his time than to the individual character of his models and, except for one or two admirable male portraits *(Whistler, Montesquiou)*, he was apt to allow the form to escape, though he excelled at indicating the tenuous and insubstantial. It cannot be said that he achieved more than a certain superficial elegance. The more rapid his work, the greater its charm. The colour reproductions made of it, on the other hand, deprived it of its original qualities of lightness and distinction.

Besides Helleu, other specialists in what was then known as 'Parisian etching' were Somm, Boutet, Gœneutte and Jeanniot, the latter of whom defies all attempts at classification. They can be dismissed as agreeable reporters. Guérard, imitator of the Japanese, devoted all his mischievous imagination and energy to the small print. Vignon specialised in fine engraving. Raffaelli produced imaginative and sympathetic studies of deserted suburbs, pieces of waste ground and small folk and their humble trades, using in turn etching, aquatint, dry point and soft-ground etching. He showed great taste and ingenuity in using colour to give a powdery effect to space without dulling the charm and sensibility of his light strokes. Chahine, author of two robust portraits of *Anatole France* and *Louise France,* nevertheless sacrificed too much to effect; he also had a weakness for picturesque, anecdotal subjects. Brouet concentrated on the world of fairs and circuses, seeking the type of beggar portrayed by Callot and Rembrandt.

The main teachings of Corot, Whistler and Seymour Haden were carried on by a French school of landscape artists whose work is characterised by the vibrative quality of their water and sky and by skilful and restrained technique. Eugène Béjot's engravings of Paris and harbour scenes, always under a clear sky, are expressed in straightforward and direct terms that show complete understanding of the potentialities of dry point used alone or with etching. Every object and surface is minutely traced, the feeling is kept under control and nothing is left to chance. Gustave Leheutre, whose art was more muted, used short, nervous strokes, softened by the burnisher. His etchings of provincial scenes, hardly bitten at all, with their silent, white spaces, look like dry points. Other members of the school were Jean-Louis Moreau, a masterly technician with perfect control over himself and his etching; Jacques Beurdeley, easily recognised by the silvery tone of his plates, which vibrate with all the sweetness and delicacy of the Ile-de-France and should entitle him to share with Chintreuil the title of painter of mists and dews; Laborde whose work was elegant and delicate; Jouas, picturesque and meticulous; Cottet, whose dramatic romanticism expressed itself in etchings which seem bitten by the sea and wind; Dauchez, faithful to his moors; Eugène Delâtre, Hercher, and many more, who are to be found represented in the portfolios of collectors who have eyes for other artists beside those of the first rank.

COPPER ENGRAVINGS BY RENOIR AND SUZANNE VALADON

Renoir never possessed a press of his own and, like Corot, only produced an occasional engraving. His first essays *(Dance in the Country,* 1890) were little more than rapid tracings. His frontispiece for Mallarmé's *Pages* (1891) reveals him in his Ingres period, tracing with fascination the detail of the breasts and stomach of *La Source.* The portrait of *Berthe Morisot, At Berneval,* the three variants of the *Pinning on Flowers,* and even more the *Two Girls Bathing* (1895), *Mother and Child,* and the two enchanting nudes with their pure sculptor's lines that adorn Duret's *Histoire des Peintres impressionnistes,* show that by then he was handling the copper with a pleasure that nothing could daunt. Despite this, however, lithography seems to have suited his genius even better.

PIERRE-AUGUSTE RENOIR. *Two Girls Bathing.* *1895.* Etching

SUZANNE VALADON. *Nude. 1895.* Soft ground etching

It was on Degas' press that, about 1895, Suzanne Valadon executed and pulled her first soft-ground etching. Degas suggested this method for her first attempt, partly because of its speed and partly because it enables the original drawing to be preserved. He knew well enough that with Suzanne there was

VINCENT VAN GOGH. *Sorrow.* *1882.* Lithograph

James Ensor. *The Cathedral*. *1886*. Etching

JAMES ENSOR. *My Portrait in 1960*. *1886*. Etching

no danger of compromise. He admired her 'hard, flexible line' which was afraid of nothing, and foresaw the harsh beauties that could not fail to come from a hand incapable of anything but the truth. And certainly the redoubtable Maria was to turn the whole process upside down. Her printer hardly knew what to make of the violent lines in the zinc which the artist had ploughed as straight as a furrow and the mordant was to bite wider and deeper still. While experts in soft-ground etching excelled at greys and light and half-tones, Suzanne Valadon's plates might have been done by a sculptor with each form given its full value, especially those of her nudes which have the hard reflections of marble.

As for the subjects, they were all of children being washed or dressed, and servant-girls washing themselves, doing their hair or lying down resting. Where Suzanne Valadon excells is in her gift for depicting the striking unity of a form. The austerity of her compositions is very different from the austerity of Degas, and what strikes one is the tone of authority; it is the strong feeling that erupts beneath the apparent coldness, the almost enforced tension; the charm, so unlike that of the average woman, a harsh, sometimes sullen charm, enriching daily life with its rough, angular violence. '*La terrible*' never drew a body that was not deformed by work or old age, her children are always ungainly. But she never tries to provoke pity and it is the stoicism of her line that never fails to move us.

After a first set of twelve zinc plates done about 1896, she did not revert to engraving until 1904 and 1905, when she did one or two dry points in which

JAMES ENSOR. *Mariakerke. 1887.* Etching

the incisions defy every rule, with great benefit to the expression. Her authoritative technique had not changed. Her numerous drawings, as well as her paintings, call for admiration of her intransigeant character and complete imperviousness to any outside influence. They are masses without a flaw, heavy; and they will last.

The only other engravers worthy to be placed beside these are Van Gogh, though he unfortunately produced only a single plate, entitled *Sorrow,* and Maurin who deserves to be better remembered as a disciple of Degas and Toulouse-Lautrec and who, together with Mary Cassatt, Pissarro *(Church and Farm at Eragny)*, Béjot, Steinlen, Lepère, Bottini, Raffaelli and Van Rysselberghe, also contributed to the revival of colour engraving.

Henri de **Toulouse-Lautrec**. *Elsa the Viennese.* *1897.* Colour lithograph

When in 1886, at the age of twenty-six, James Ensor made his first essays on copper and zinc, he had already painted his masterpieces *Still-life with Cabbage,* the *Middle-class Home, The Skate, Girl eating Oysters, Scandalised Masks,* and others. His engravings, of which he did over a hundred and fifty, were inspired by the same determination not to be the slave of either his observation or his fantasy. He resembled his predecessors, Bresdin and Redon, in never allowing himself to be led away by his attraction towards the ridiculous and the macabre. Just as Redon's lithographed portraits explain how it was that he could create credible monsters, so Ensor's portraits—his own, and those of his father and *Ernest Rousseau*—as well as numerous little landscapes, down-to-earth, life-like and bathed in light, such as the *Orchard,* the *Main Harbour at Ostend, Boats on the Beach* or *Mariakerke,* show that he can achieve nobility without introducing any of that semi-contemptuous picturesque element which was only one of the fields in which he excelled.

Other of his works included a number of slight plates in the same vein as the famous *Seven Deadly Sins,* but these are only diversions which seem trivial when put beside the epic buffoonery and immense verve of Bruegel, Goya, Daumier or even Rowlandson. Ensor's genius did not lie in the direction of satire. Neither *The Constables, Just Judges, Gamesters, The Quacks* nor *The Old Rascals* are more than farce. His breezy fancy may liven up various over-populated compositions like *Battle of the Golden Spurs, Bathing at Ostend,* or *Devils thrashing Angels and Archangels,* but these agreeable drawings are only the toys of a god who likes sometimes to put off his dignity.

But the toys ceased to be amusing when, guided by his familiar demon (he once said that instead of an angel he had a guardian devil), and suddenly possessed by fears or dark forebodings, he sees himself surrounded by doors opening on to mystery. This tendency towards the supernatural had appeared already in various small, and at first sight realistic, plates such as *The Haunted Cabinet, The Street Lamp, The House on the Boulevard Anspach, Coppice at Groenendal* or *Stars above the Cemetery.* In these, for certain very fine and lightly bitten strokes, the point has been used with a brief and sudden precision recalling that of creaks that punctuate a sleepless night. Strange acolytes, escaped from some cemetery or kermesse, suddenly take up their residence in the studio, addressing each other in the meaningless phrases of ghosts. But none of the feverish little devils (puppets rather than ghosts) that plague the artist seem at bottom very alarming. A laughing or grotesque mask hides the face of an inoffensive old man, or of a triumphant or defeated fool, and we often wonder whether what we are looking at is a mask or a real face.

Many of Ensor's etchings, as, for example, *Skeletons warming themselves* or *Skeleton in the Studio,* are done after paintings, and are inspired by the same irony discovered in the unusual. In others, the fantasy is more specific; some legend or great text has served as a spring-board for the artist's imagination, as in the justly celebrated *The Revenge of Hop-Frog, King Plague* and the magnificent set from the New Testament: *Christ calming the Storm, Christ beset by Devils,* or *Christ's entry into Brussels* in which, as in *The Cathedral,* the whole city is shown swarming with people in the manner of the Flemish school. To quote Verhaeren: 'Pressed compactly together, in its thousands, a multitude advances, not with its arms, legs or bodies, but with its faces, towards an unknown goal. Is it for some colossal fête, some prodigious anniversary? It is an epic spectacle... The etching might be the work of a tribe of flies or a swarm of insects.'

After 1904, Ensor ceased to produce engravings; but he was to continue to have a profound influence on the new generation of Belgian artists whose surrealism, instead escaping into vague ideologies, has always had a solid basis.

THE RENAISSANCE OF BLACK AND WHITE AND COLOUR LITHOGRAPHY

About 1890 lithography, which had continued to be practised by Fantin-Latour and Redon, suddenly returned to fashion. This was partly due to the publication, one after the other, of Roger-Marx's *L'Estampe originale* and Vollard's *Peintres-Graveurs.* What was new was that it was now colour lithography by which artists were attracted. Fascinated by Chéret's posters and by Japanese prints, they were discovering that the rich colours of their palettes could be reproduced on wood, copper or stone.

The example had been given in 1874 by Manet with his *Punchinello,* which he had done after a water-colour by using seven stones. But there can be no doubt that the real initiator was Jules Chéret. In his hands, the colour which his predecessors had misused in their posters and married so cruelly with their blacks, was at last to retrieve its charm and freedom. Long before he had worked out the rules of chromo-lithography, Chéret had instinctively used colour with the crayon. His high-lights in wash seem scattered by accident, but are added with the surest of touches. The composition is skilful and as rich as the distribution of the values. In the same way, thanks to use of successive stones, large flat reds, blues, yellows and oranges form a contrast with the light touches of crayon, spatter and transparent hatchings. It is to these oppositions between filled and unfilled spaces that his pictures owe their solidity and their depth. Subsequently he gave up indicating contours altogether, relying solely on the contrast between dark and light, cold and warmth, to indicate them sufficiently. The forms became no more than a charming pretext for the colours to balance or contrast with each other.

HENRI DE TOULOUSE-LAUTREC. *Dancing at the Moulin-Rouge. 1897.*
Colour lithograph

Chéret allowed his imagination free rein in his instinctive knowledge of contrasting and complementary colours. A friend of the great Impressionists, he forestalled Seurat in guessing the laws of divisionism and delivered lithography from its former monotony to make it an art. He and the Japanese engravers together emancipated the eyes of the painters. On this point, Puvis de Chavannes' work offers the most convincing evidence, with that of Toulouse-Lautrec and the younger generation of artists like Bonnard, Vuillard, Roussel, Denis and Signac who had their work printed by Clot around 1895.

Many of the colour plates published by Vollard owe a considerable amount to the printer, and are little more than first class facsimiles of Renoir, Sisley, Cézanne or Guillaumin. But many others, such as Redon's *The Shulamite Woman* and *Beatrice,* Vuillard's *Landscapes* and *Interiors, Aspects of Parisian Life* by Bonnard, and a number of the sets which Roussel, Maurice Denis, Dulac, Signac and Luce were commissioned to produce, are genuinely original work, and so too were the more anecdotal plates produced by artists like Lewis Brown or Lunois. A few colour etchings also appeared but, despite the undoubted success of Mary Cassatt, Pissarro, Maurin and Bottini in this line, it soon proved to present considerably more risks than colour lithography. The process of etching is already sufficiently complicated without adding to it the difficulty of preparing the colours, which is apt to distract the artist's attention from what is far more important, the placing of his lines and the choice of ink and paper. In colour etching the predominant role is that of the printer and the method of colouring *à la poupée* takes the place of the use of several plates; the tone loses its boldness, the 'white spaces cease to have any *raison d'être* and the etching is ruined by having tried to emulate a painting. Thus it was that, in spite of Raffaelli's enthusiasm which led him, in 1904, to found the *Salon de l'eau-forte en couleurs,* and although certain successful colour etchings were achieved, the process soon declined into a mere vehicle for cheap reproductions. The use of wood blocks for colour engraving, however, goes back for centuries and we shall see later on the use that Henri Rivière, Lepère, Gauguin and the Beltrands were able to make of it.

Many of the coloured lithographs of this period are exquisite pieces of work to which we shall be returning later, but true connoisseurs have always preferred the black and white. It was a happy combination of circumstances that led masters like Toulouse-Lautrec, Degas, Renoir, Rodin, Gauguin, Forain, Maillol, Vuillard and Bonnard, between 1890 and 1900, to devote to lithography so large a share of their time and invention.

THE LITHOGRAPHS OF TOULOUSE-LAUTREC

Together with those of Daumier, these lithographs form the most magnificent body of work on stone that we possess. It may seem exaggerated to find points of comparison between two men so totally different in origin, upbringing and

HENRI DE TOULOUSE-LAUTREC. *Jockey coming up to the Post.* *c. 1895.*
Lithograph

temperament. But for each of them, all that was most ordinary and earthly in him was the object of a curiosity so intense as to give to reality the proportions of a dream; and it was a dream in which Toulouse-Lautrec spent his all too brief life. Between 1892 and 1900 he produced nearly four hundred plates, of which about fifty were coloured, and he would no doubt have gone on to produce as many as Daumier himself. Like the latter, he had an exceptionally good visual memory, an indispensable possession for a lithographer who cannot carry his stone about with him and must therefore compose from memory if he wishes to avoid the deadening effect of tracing or transfer. Toulouse-Lautrec looked and remembered, and his memory sharpened and refined his recollections. He was never working more freely than when he was bending over his stone at Stern's or Ancourt's, silent and far from any model; the surface under his hand far more receptive than the marble of the café tables from which so many of his drawings were wiped away by the waiter's cloth.

It would be a mistake to do what has been too lightly and too often done before, and try to compare Toulouse-Lautrec with Degas. Throughout a long and well-protected life, Degas never ceased studying the technique of painting which Lautrec practised almost by instinct, and, while Degas' drawing remained for a long time under the influence of the earlier masters, Lautrec's did so to a far less degree. It is curious that the idea has persisted for so long that Toulouse-Lautrec wanted to revenge himself on Nature for his deformity, as though his taste for what was ugly had obscured the nobility of his character. He analysed, he did not chronicle; he was a poet, not a satirist. Unlike Forain, he had no wish to display human wickedness. He did not use light and shade to help him draw attention to what was odious in an individual or a situation, nor did he feel, like Degas, a need to pollute what was enchanting or add contempt and hatred to the wonderful. With him, each drawing was an act of adoration. He was delighted by everything that concerns man; every manifestation of character, however exaggerated, filled him with wonder and exaltation. It has never been sufficiently stressed that what fascinated him as he hurried wildly up and down the streets from one bar or theatre, one *maison close* to another, was man's inner life. In reality, his pictures are not so far from portraits. In the human comedy he was creating, he did not content himself with a few elementary characters and stock situations. There is always a touch of the particular to enliven the general. With his infinite respect for the individual, what concerned him was the conditions chance had put men in, their callings, the deformations old age or circumstances had forced on them. He selected his observation posts to catch his models going about their daily tasks not knowing they were observed, that they might reveal simultaneously their most fleeting and most durable characteristics.

But it would be to misunderstand the essence of Lautrec's work to judge it only by the picturesque element that both colours and dates it. Forgetting for a moment the theatres and music-halls, the red saloons, all the scenery and accessories, let us try to realise how much more complex than we imagined are the dancers, actresses or prostitutes from whom he liked to choose his models.

HENRI DE TOULOUSE-LAUTREC. *Sleep. 1896.* Lithograph

With the skill that makes everything clear, alive and lovable—in the widest sense of the word—he showed us the source from which this smile, that turn of the head, these bows and those silences were made.

Toulouse-Lautrec made his name with his very first posters (1892): *La Goulue at the Moulin-Rouge, Le Pendu, The Japanese Divan, Bruant, Reine de Joie* and the rest. They were his initiation into drawing on stone, which Chéret's light-hearted genius was already using to decorate the walls of Paris. At the same time as his lively and attractive posters, the Japanese prints were continuing their assault upon the conventions. They made a principle of asymmetry; the climax of a composition was off-centre. They paid no attention to the traditional interplay of shadow and sunlight. Their bold and delicate colouring and composition, and their respect for daily routine and humble objects exercised a fascination to

Henri de Toulouse-Lautrec. *A la Souris. c. 1895.* Lithograph

which Lautrec in due course succumbed. He began by producing colour lithographs of which the early ones are almost posters (*La Goulue and her Sister, Englishman at the Moulin-Rouge*), but he soon realised that the broad effects that constitute the attraction of the plates signed in 1893 and the vivid contrasts permissible in mural decoration were not suitable for smaller compositions destined to be looked at from nearer at hand.

The covers he did in 1893 for *Vieilles Histoires,* in black and white, still have something of the poster and of Hokusai's ink drawings. The contours are put in with the brush and dramatic blacks contrast with vigorous whites standing out against a spatter background. Soon however, the brush lines are accompanied by the more delicate and vigorous lines of the crayon. As in Bonnard's and Vuillard's work, we see the gradual reappearance of the form where before there had only been patches. The *Café-concert* and *The Skirmish* sets show an increasing use of spatter. Lautrec's first portrait of Yvette Guilbert already shows all the characteristics of his work; it is a simple profile in which, by varying the intensity of his line, he has successfully indicated all the planes of the face. *En Quarante* shows a similar lightness of touch. By reducing the amount of stopping-out, lightening his shadows and clarifying the spatter with the help of the toothbrush he always carried with him, he let fall here and there the silvery luminous rain that shadows the face of Oenone and makes Phaedra's face stand out as white as marble (*Sarah Bernhardt*). With his crayon he would add a small, carefully-calculated touch of black to a lip, a lock of hair, a bow on a dress, the tip of a shoe. Almost all these plates take their inspiration from either the stage or the promenade of the Théâtre-Français, Théâtre Libre, Folies-Bergère, Moulin-Rouge or Gaieté-Rochechouart.

He was probably to some extent influenced by Whistler's lithographs. The sight of these little masterpieces, made up of the slightest of strokes and hardly inked, tenuous but nevertheless precise, did not lead him to abandon the use of brush and wash for his highlights, but it did teach him to use them with discretion. To depict all the roles of an Yvette Guilbert or a Marcelle Lender, Lautrec sharpened up his vision. Any comic element likely to unbalance the picture can be said to be transfigured by the sensuous pleasure he finds in the drawing of a look, smile, shoulder, a hand or back, a gesture, step, or dance, or suggesting the fragile miracle that can be created by the body of an actress or ballerina absorbed in her part. The brilliant transposition of lines and values on to the stone in itself is a miracle. Half-seas over in her little top-hat, letting the chorus drop from the corner of her mouth as though it were an insult, *Cécy Loftus* enchants us by the many truths of every kind of which she is the expression.

Toulouse-Lautrec took infinite care over the quality of his stones and the choice of paper and his grey-green, grey-brown and grey-black inks, in order that no accident should mar these masterpieces. It is almost as though he thought the 'beautiful blacks' dear to lithographers and the contrasts between these velvet surfaces and the pure whites that are the pride of the romantics too easy. It was in this spirit of sobriety that he embarked on the *Portraits of Actors and Actresses,* and the 1896 series of masterpieces of which the prototype is the plate

Henri de Toulouse-Lautrec. *Cécy Loftus.* *1895.* Lithograph

showing *Ida Heath* in her *tutu,* her left leg flung up above her head and her two arms falling back, Ida Heath graceful, intent and happy, her blonde hair and fluttering tulle emphasised by the dead black of her bodice and the little knots on her shoulders, leading her scintillating dance. *The Box* (Faust), *Supper in London, Black and White* all deserve description as masterpieces of movement and economy of line in which the slightest stroke tells and has its own value, almost its own scent.

The same year (1896) saw the beginning of an important body of work in which colour was once again to predominate. But these are very different from his first lithographs, for Toulouse-Lautrec knew now that in colour lithography, as in black and white, it is possible to express everything even with limited means. He no longer used a brush except very lightly to strengthen a contour or add density to a surface; the structure of the drawing remains visible through the fine, iridescent spatter. In place of the bold outlines and flat tints of earlier work, there is the impalpable vibration produced by the scattering of minute drops, between which sparkles the white of the paper. This was Toulouse-Lautrec's substitute for the dots of 'divisionism', as Pissarro's was the grain of aquatint. It is impossible to praise too highly not only the quality of harmonies which had already appeared in his posters and theatre programmes, but also the discretion with which he introduces his highlights, as though he already foresaw the misuse that would later be made of them by so many engravers who had come under his influence. The most striking plates of the *Elles* set may well be those which, like *Lassitude,* are printed in a single tone. This set, however, designed to show woman's life in her home, had already been preceded by another masterpiece, *Sleep,* in which we can almost feel the model's breath and in which the line of face and breast, and even of the hands, is so pure that it recalls both the drawings of the 18th century—especially as the colour is that of sanguine—and the most perfect delineations of the female form ever made in Venice or Ancient Greece. The year 1897 saw the production of *The Grand Box at the Theatre, Female Clown at the Moulin-Rouge, Princely Idyll, Dancing at the Moulin-Rouge, The Small Box* and *The Picnic Party,* in which the concision of the harmonies reaches a point of perfection unequalled in the colour prints of any other country, except possibly Japan. This concision is matched by that of the analysis and the line which Toulouse-Lautrec himself never surpassed afterwards except in his wonderful portrait of *Elsa the Viennese.*

But at the same time he was producing other lithographs, equally good, that owed nothing to colour. *A la Souris* is one, and here for the first time a dog appears in the foreground. Hitherto dogs had not been frequent in his pictures but from now onwards bulldogs, poodles and fox terriers constantly appear alongside his horses and human beings. His vigorous set of lithographs of equestrian scenes *(The Paddock, Jockey coming up to the Post, The Trainer, Riding Habit and Governess Cart, The Aged Horse,* to name some of them), produced shortly before the onset of the troubles that were to end his life, show his limitless understanding of everything that lives and breathes. They have a classical directness and simplicity.

PIERRE-AUGUSTE RENOIR. *Pinning on Flowers*. Colour lithograph

It is easy to imagine what Toulouse-Lautrec might have achieved had not his work been cut short by death. Anything and everything served to excite his imagination, and he gave it free rein even if only designing a book cover, the title page for a piece of music or an invitation card. Now, however, all this was to be enriched by a new element. There are many signs that he was looking for fresh subjects; that he was on the point of abandoning his place in the theatre and at the café table. In the illustrations he was commissioned to do for *Histoires naturelles* he brings to his pictures of the life of animals something of the poetry of the elements. He displays in them the keen vision of a Jules Renard and something of the simplicity of La Fontaine. His sudden outbursts of impishness or eroticism, issuing in numberless little extempore sketches, are still there, but it seems as though a new seriousness was taking hold of him. I am not now thinking only of the *Faces of Actresses* that he did about 1898, but of that most admirable of all his portraits, *Au Hanneton,* of the woman whom pleasure has wrung dry, eternally riveted, it seems, to the bench on which she sits, staring quietly in front of her and yet still finding the courage to smile through her froth of tulle and feathers. By what miracle has the artist succeeded in maintaining that wonderful powdery, silver tone, with the single touch of black provided by the little dog sitting faithfully beside his mistress?

Toulouse-Lautrec's lithographs are the expression *par excellence* of the French genius. They were the most balanced and the subtlest example of wit, observation and taste that had appeared since Fragonard. Some engravings are no more than an experiment or amusement for the artist who does them. Toulouse-Lautrec's too may be called an amusement but they are a basic one. As though to accentuate their aristocratic character they were only printed in small numbers, but they are at the centre of an immense body of work, of a magnificence that was only tardily acknowledged.

THE PORTRAITS OF EUGENE CARRIÈRE

RENOIR, GAUGUIN AND MAILLOL'S LITHOGRAPHS

When he was a young man, Carrière worked for a commercial lithographer, as the title-pages of various novels still bear witness. It was not until about 1890 that he took up engraving again. Even an early plate, like *Infant in a Bonnet,* shows the beginnings of the technique later perfected in his great portraits. It is one based on erasure, using scraper, glass-paper, crayon and ink wash, and the effect is not unlike a mezzotint. *Alphonse Daudet* and his daughters *Nelly, Elise* and *Marguerite, Edmond de Goncourt, Verlaine, Rochefort, Puvis de Chavannes* emerge from the shadows, without it being possible to say where the light on their faces comes from and whether they themselves are not its source. The outlines of mouth and eyes are indicated by touches of the crayon that are hardly more than shadows on wax or marble and yet reveal the finest subtleties of their planes with a precision worthy of a sculptor.

194

PIERRE-AUGUSTE RENOIR. *Portrait of Wagner. c. 1885.* Lithograph

EUGÈNE CARRIÈRE. *Portrait of Marguerite Carrière. c. 1895.* Lithograph

What Carrière was seeking was a way of reproducing the play of light and shade on which he was now concentrating in his painting. With the help of his printer Duchâtel, he discovered it by adopting the method of successive impressions. The first impression was transferred to a second stone and then printed in a more sustained tone. In this way, he was able to produce the blacks that contrast with the transparent greys he achieved with the aid of the scraper or cloth. His heads stand out against a dark background or, more accurately, are a part of the background which is itself a living thing, a link between matter and spirit, the sole source of energy and movement. Without ever imprisoning his forms by contours, Carrière had the power of conveying

EUGÈNE CARRIÈRE. *Portrait of Paul Verlaine. 1896.* Lithograph

individual character in a forehead, a temple, a cheek or an eyebrow, so that
although he shows us only the face and the whole emphasis is thus on mental
characteristics, we feel we know the whole figure. 'Builder' *(constructeur)*,
the catch-phrase ignorantly bandied about for the past forty years, can rightly
be applied to the author of the lithograph portraits of *Verlaine* or *Lisbeth,* as to
Cézanne or Seurat.

Carrière abandoned interest in the sensual aspect of things as in everything
that detracted from his main subject. No artist ever carried to greater lengths
the art of sacrificing the inessential, and no portraits achieve a greater depth
of meaning than his.

PIERRE-AUGUSTE RENOIR. *Child with a Biscuit*. Lithograph

PAUL GAUGUIN. *Manao Tupapau. 1889.* Lithograph

Renoir's lithographs *(Diéterle* or *Lady in a Picture Hat, Wagner, Rodin, Cézanne, Pierre Renoir as a Child)*, done more hastily and in many cases after his own paintings, have a charm that is irresistibile. Even more than the large coloured lithographs reproduced by Clot *(Girl Bathing,* the two *Pinning on Flowers, Children playing Ball* and *Child with a Biscuit)*, which, despite a vibrative quality like that of a pastel, remain no more than interpretations, these portraits with their light, brilliant touch and their subtle tint added by the brush, have a sensitivity that could only come from Renoir. They have a sensual vigour such that they practically compose themselves. There is a richness in their masses and flexibility in their movement, in other words a perfect blending of inner and surface truth, by which the artist has succeeded in capturing the most fleeting charms and giving a look of permanence to even the most impromptu plate.

In about 1889, Gauguin produced a set of lithographs on yellow paper, inspired by his paintings of Martinique, Pont-Aven and Arles. These, made on zinc plates and earlier than his wood engravings, are characteristic of his *'synthétiste'* period with their large flat surfaces and deliberately hard outlines. They have less distinction than *Manao Tupapau* which he produced between two

PIERRE PUVIS DE CHAVANNES. *Normandy*. *1893*. Lithograph

visits to Tahiti and which appeared in *L'Estampe originale*. This other, dark, Olympia, the modelling of her body indicated by erasings, lies in a framework alive with mysterious points of light that recall a lithograph by Redon. Every quality of the stone contributes to this composition, which was Gauguin's last lithograph, except for one line drawing inspired by a Maori girl. In his subsequent admirable work on wood, it will be seen how he still continued to think in terms of lithography.

It is to be regretted that Puvis de Chavannes did not produce a greater number of lithographs. *Normandy, Young Girl in a Picture Hat*, and particularly the transfer drawing entitled *The Poor Fisherman* show how admirably adapted stone was to the nobility and serenity of his grey tones.

Another incomparable lithograph is Rodin's *New Idol* which is later than his dry points. His illustrations for the *Jardin des Supplices* were largely watercolours transferred to stone, but in *New Idol* two forms inter-penetrate each other, as do the light and shade. This unique plate, which shows the sculptor of *The Kiss* obtaining effects similar to those of Carrière's lithograph of *Verlaine*, is a testimony to the friendship that united these two artists.

One or two wood-engravings and lithographs by Aristide Maillol, showing the influence of both Renoir and the Symbolists, appeared around 1895 and gave an indication of the unity of form later to distinguish his sculpture.

WHISTLER'S LITHOGRAPHS

Like many Americans, Whistler began by considering lithography as one of the inferior forms of engraving. It was not until 1878 or 1879 that the printer Thomas Way, who was responsible for re-awakening interest in lithography in England, induced him to execute his first set of sixteen lithographs. These, for which he chose the modest title of 'Notes', included a *Nocturne in Blue*, a *View of the Thames, Limehouse* and the *Victoria and Albert Docks*. After that, he abandoned lithography again for eight years, but came back to it on discovering in transfer paper a useful means of preserving an impromptu air in even the most carefully thought-out compositions.

The dangers of using transfer paper, and the likelihood of its producing characterless prints, have been already referred to. But Whistler, with his miraculous lightness of touch, his desire to suggest rather than describe and to express only the very essence of what he saw, succeeded in producing wonderful greys by the lightest of pressures on white paper with the tip of the crayon. The seventy prints he now produced were characterised by the economy of means employed. Within their small compass they summarise all that is most delicate in the work of an artist who never allows himself to become affected.

The plates he produced during 1895 and 1896, many of then views from his room looking over the Thames *(Little London, Savoy Pigeons)*, others of other parts of London or interiors *(Kensington Gardens, The Siesta, The Balcony)*, others again showing blacksmiths' shops, stables, inns, are as good as any he had done in Paris a few years before (*The Luxemburg Gardens, Confidences, The Grande Galerie in the Louvre* or *The Lazy Beauty*). He never felt himself younger or more free than when he was depicting young girls, like Tanagra figurines, as in *Young Model Reading,* or *Seated Nude* reproduced in *L'Estampe originale.* Even his most celebrated portraits in oils do not show a greater delicacy of touch than his lithograph portraits of Sickert, Pennell or Mallarmé. The last of these, who also sat for Manet, Munch and Vallotton, said of his portrait by Whistler: 'It is wonderful; the only real study that has ever been made of me and I am smiling at myself.' It is a masterpiece in which the artist's subtlety and that of the writer seems to merge, and it well deserves the description 'poem on stone' that Whistler gave to several of his plates.

When he experimented with polychrome, Whistler followed Toulouse-Lautrec in the discretion with which he used it, contrary to public taste and the practice of nearly all the other colour-etchers of the period. His little coloured lithographs (*Yellow House at Lannion, Red House at Paimpol, View of the Thames, Reclining Nude*) prove, as later those of Vuillard, that it is often the greatest economy of means that produces the richest effects.

Whistler devoted the same care as Toulouse-Lautrec to the choice of paper and of frames for his prints. It was certainly he who brought about the revival of original lithography at the end of the last century, especially in his own country with the work of Ricketts, Shannon, Belleroche and Conder. His Propositions on painting are equally valid for engraving : To catch life, one must be as quick as life itself...A work on which much earnest labour has been spent should appear as though done quickly and without effort...A picture is finished when all trace of the means used to bring about the end has disappeared.

BONNARD, VUILLARD, ROUSSEL, MAURICE DENIS

Bonnard who, at the time, was experimenting in every direction—posters, furniture, screens, stage scenery—became attracted by lithography at about the same time as Toulouse-Lautrec. His first poster, *France-Champagne,* was printed by Ancourt. It recalls the work of Chéret and of other prints in which the Japanese influence is revealed by the unusualness of the composition and the freshness of the tones, laid on flat and without outlines. His *Domestic Scenes,* a set of small lithographs illustrating nineteen of Claude Terrasse's songs, are less pleasing on account of the abbreviations and distortions they contain. But, in spite of this, these illustrations, and those he did for the same writer's *Petit Solfège,* have nevertheless a genuinely new plastic and poetic quality. They are done with pen and brush and succeed in re-creating the form and giving a fresh look to figures as well as to objects or landscapes (*Grandfather's Song, The Morning Angelus, Dreams, Woman Rider,* etc.). Bonnard was later to abandon the distortion and the broken effects to which, notwithstanding, his earlier work owes

JAMES MCNEILL WHISTLER. *Draped seated figure.* *1893.* Lithograph

James McNeill Whistler. *Portrait of Mallarmé.* *1893.* Lithograph

PIERRE BONNARD. *Dogs. c. 1900.* Lithograph

EDOUARD VUILLARD. *Portrait of Paul Léautaud.* Lithograph

a part of its charm *(Dogs, Nude).* Other lithographs of his first period include a set for *L'Œuvre* and the covers for *Le Théâtre des Pantins* and Mellerio's *La Lithographie en couleurs.*

In 1900 appeared Verlaine's *Parallèlement,* for so long neglected by the bibliophiles. The freedom with which its margins were scattered with arabesques, filling up every free space, seemed at the time as outrageous as the text itself. Since the period of the Romantics and Delacroix's *Faust,* it had been rare for lithography to be used for book illustrations and only the publishers of *Au pied du Sinaï* and later of *Histoires Naturelles* had had the courage to demonstrate how well the process was suited to typography. Bonnard took an almost childish delight in these vivacious drawings, in which the use made of the point of the

EDOUARD VUILLARD. *The Game of Draughts.* Colour lithograph

crayon, and the light flat surfaces give a pleasure not unlike that produced by
the work of Whistler or Toulouse-Lautrec. They might be described as illustrations in verse, following with ease the rhythm of each poem.

Daphnis and Chloé (1902) and *Parallèlement* are two of the most beautiful of the
illustrated books published since the 18th century. The former, particularly,
is an extraordinary out-pouring of genius and it is amazing that Bonnard should
have taken less than a year to compose these hundred and sixty lithographs, each
in its own little frame, following the text so closely and depicting sea and landscapes, harbours, squares, rooms in farms or palaces, figures, clothed or uncloth-
ed, playing the flute surrounded by dogs and flocks of sheep or engaged in
the duet whose prelude is the subject of the book. Bonnard succeeds without

Edouard Vuillard. *Portrait of Cézanne.* Colour lithograph

difficulty in evoking the scenes of antiquity and the light of happier times. In various earlier works, his sense of fun had betrayed his drawing into a certain complexity, but now it took on a poise of which he might previously have been judged incapable. The *Daphnis* lithographs foreshadow to some extent the paintings of his mature period, where, master by then of his technique, he could afford to depict those adorable movements to which his preoccupation with the colour he had re-discovered sometimes led him to sacrifice his forms. His technique in these lithographs forms part of their attraction and enhances their charm. *Daphnis* was received with the same lack of appreciation as both *Parallèlement* and the set of colour lithographs entitled *Some Aspects of Paris Life*, in which the artist, for whom such commonplace objects as a horse, a dog, or a hat represented so many enigmas, depicts with delight the picturesque incidents and background of a great city. The set shows us the Paris bridges and boulevards under rain and snow, the teeming streets seen from the fifth floor of some building, the occupants of the pit seen from the dress circle. A few plates depict the pleasures of boating or the sea-green of gardens. In these prints, some of which appeared in the portfolio of the *Peintres-graveurs*, Bonnard's powers of transfiguring what he saw reached their height. But so little were they understood at the time that, like most of his friends, he gave up illustration and engraving altogether.

Vuillard's early lithographs *(The Kitchen, The Window)* indicate his favourite choice of subject. They date from 1893 but were never printed. Not long afterwards we find him producing a set of small ornamental lithographs for the catalogue of the *Dépêche* exhibition—at which he was also exhibiting, alongside Bonnard, Anquetin, Maurin and Sérusier—as well as for the supplements of the *Revue blanche* and various numbers of the *Epreuve*. Done in crayon and wash, they testify to the poetry to be found in little bourgeois interiors, women trying on hats, laying tables, all shown in a kindly half-light. In the charming programmes he designed for Lugné-Poe, the text, written with the brush, itself provides an additional and unexpected ornament. Whether out of modesty or a fear lest he should be wasting his talent, Vuillard never consented to illustrate a book. It is a pity. Of all artists, his gifts of analysis, his meticulousness and the care he gave to reproducing the spirit of a period would seem to have marked him out for such a task. It is a pity, too, that he did not follow the example of Odilon Redon and Renoir and give us lithograph portraits like those he did in oils.

In addition to his monochrome prints with their rich blacks and variegated greys achieved by use of the scraper *(The Box at the Theatre, Rehearsal at the Œuvre)*, Vuillard also published about twenty colour plates. The flat tint of the background, with its matt or sustained tones, is emphasised here and there with light touches of the crayon. The artist has returned to the Western concept of a print. The abbreviations to be seen in his early experiments, the large flat areas introduced with the brush, everything that smacked too much of the poster, have all disappeared. Vuillard brought back to the small print the feeling of depth and the play of light and shade. Broken tones abound; pinkish and golden

MAURICE DENIS. *Les Attitudes sont faciles et chastes.* Lithograph

greys, light and dark browns, slate greys, contrast with accents of clean colour. Some of the set of twelve plates published by him in 1898 depict bustling life in modest homes. These are an example of everything that is most exquisite and most profound in Vuillard's art, but unhappily he did not follow them up. Instead he abandoned engraving for a considerable period, like Bonnard or Roussel, whose unpublished set of landscapes, as light and airy as pastels, vibrate with greens, yellows and tender pinks enhanced by the white areas here and there; like Maurice Denis, whose portfolio *Amours* with its straightforward mysticism is, with Dulac's *Song of Songs,* an essential document for the study of the symbolist period in engraving; like Henri Rivière, who, with the help of his printer, Verneau, and by using the roller to tone down his light and shade, succeeded in obtaining effects recalling those of his coloured wood-cuts *(Aspects of Nature, Paris Townscapes, The Fairyland of Hours, Thirty-six Views of the Eiffel Tower)* ; like Vallotton, Luce, Signac, Cross, Anquetin, d'Espagnat, Ranson, Seguin, Charles Guérin or the charming and talented Serret, all of whose excursions into lithography were only too brief. Quite suddenly, the colour lithograph movement, whose history was brilliantly summarised by Mellerio, came to an end. As for black and white lithography, except for Redon's admirable portraits, a few figures by Belleroche, Guiguet, Henri Bataille, J.-E. Blanche, Ernest Laurent and Aman-Jean, a few landscapes by Le Sidaner and the productions of the comic artists, there are no great names to represent the years between 1900 and 1917.

LITHOGRAPHS AND ETCHINGS BY FORAIN

It was about 1890 that Jean-Louis Forain first took up lithography. Up till then, his only engraved work had been his frontispieces for *Marthe* and the plates he had done for the *Croquis Parisiens* (1880). Very soon, like Whistler, he began printing his own plates, giving careful attention to his inks and papers, with the result that we possess, for each plate, of which in any case he never took more than fifty impressions and sometimes only numbers varying from two to fifteen, a series of prints showing considerable variations. The fashion for him in America has concentrated on his etchings. The French view, on the other hand, is that he produced no better expressions of his own temperament and his period than the beautiful sets that can be classified under *Private Rooms, Boxes at the Theatre, The Wings, Toilettes, Court Scenes* and *Strike Scenes.* With an undoubted sense of movement, and great skill at cutting-out (in every sense, including that most often given to the term by women) a scene, Forain, like Mirbeau for whom he would have been the perfect illustrator, reduces humanity to one or two striking types, without much depth of character. Three or four backcloths are all he needs to stage his scenes. And he often repeats a theme like a man revolving an old grievance. For example, there are no fewer than ten versions of *Massage after the Bath.*

EDOUARD VUILLARD. *The Cook. 1899.* Colour lithograph

Jean-Louis Forain. *At the Restaurant. c. 1900.* Lithograph

He draws like a fighter; a blow here, an insult there. The chiaroscuro of which Daumier, followed by Carrière, made so much use, Forain uses as though it were a go-between, whose sole aim is to foster enmity and misunderstanding. Nevertheless, his compositions are undeniably powerful and provide a detailed picture of manners and habits at the turn of the century. How quickly they have disappeared, Forain's journalists like Arthur Meyer, artists, bewhiskered business men with moustaches and corporations, chewing cigars and not to be separated from their top hats, brief-cases and umbrellas! His women are all hunted creatures selling themselves without pleasure. The accessories which in Toulouse-Lautrec's work have the prettiness of something in a Japanese house (the dressing-gown, towel, scent bottles, soap, hair-brush, tooth-brush—everything that in *Elles* is adorable, the bath-tub equally with the armchair or the mantlepiece), in Forain looks stale and unfriendly. In Degas, an enchanted

JEAN-LOUIS FORAIN. *Lady at her Toilet with her Maid.* *c. 1900.* Lithograph

light illuminates the stage and the movements of the dancers; in Forain, an air
of poverty and the monotony of a calling to which no shred of illusion still
attaches lies over the whole theatre, in the wings and boxes alike. Even in his
later work, where his purpose is more serious, such as *Strike Scenes,*
with its speaker urging on the crowd of working-men from the top of a stand,
In Greece (1897) with its pictures of the devastation caused by war that are the
forerunners of the moving series done in 1914-1918, or *Court Scenes* with the fat
guard holding back the public, the mother and children who have lost their case;
even in these we are repelled by the lack of sympathy and the craving to debase
everything; the '*lyrisme au vitriol*', the corrosive imagination that also characterises the work of Mirbeau, Bloy and Taillade. In spite of this, Forain's lithographs
are among the most powerful of the century. The impetuous lines, often broken
and angular, the bad temper that makes the parallel hatchings look like a row
of insults, the art with which the shadows are grouped round the forms, the threat-
ening atmosphere, make these lithographs superior to any of his pen or brush
work, and show how much he had gained since his early drawings.

THÉOPHILE-ALEXANDRE STEINLEN. *The Grandfather.* Etching

THÉOPHILE-ALEXANDRE STEINLEN. *Tramps in the Snow.* Lithograph

We do not know what inspired him to take up again the etching he had not touched since his early experiments in *Marthe*. This time, without abandoning the themes of his lithographs, he was trying for a more naturalistic atmosphere. The masters he followed were to be first, Degas and Toulouse-Lautrec, and then Rembrandt and Daumier; none of whom however succeeded in teaching him even a measure of tolerance, let alone any kindness. Now that he was approaching old age he sought the consolations of religion in the Bible. But all he could find there was one more 'story', the history of a trial, a 'case'. He could depict the traitor, the executioner, the impenitent thief; but the face of Christ eluded him.

But the nobler style to which Forain now aspired is still not without its contrivances. To enhance the dramatic appeal of a scene he overloads it, slashes it with arbitrary hatchings; and as he works over his plates, the candour of the earlier states recedes further and further. Nevertheless, etchings such as *After*

MAX KLINGER. *Early Spring*. Etching and aquatint

the Vision, unforgettable with its great unfilled space in the centre, *Meeting under the Dome*, *The Breaking of Bread*, or the sets inspired by *The Prodigal Son*, show how he struggled to find better sources of strength than violence and bitterness.

The rarity of his etchings, of which very few impressions were taken, explains the demand there has been for them. Forain will live by his engraved work, rather than by his paintings in which melodramatic lighting effects are used to give an unreal pathos to characterless figures.

THE HUMORISTS: WILLETTE, STEINLEN, LÉANDRE, JEAN VÉBER

Original lithography had gradually disappeared from the satirical publications in which it had come to its original flowering, having been killed by the new

MAX LIEBERMANN. *The Weaver. c. 1883.* Etching

MAX LIEBERMANN. *Bathers.* *c.* *1885.* Etching

photo-mechanical processes. The era of the Daumiers and Gavarnis seemed at an end and political caricature abandoned once for all. The Dreyfus Case was to arouse fierce controversy, but for Forain, Caran d'Ache, Steinlen and Hermann Paul, whichever side they fought on, the greasy crayon was only an occasional weapon. It is infinitely regrettable, as so many critics have remarked, that their ephemeral productions for the daily or weekly papers should have been coarsened by stereotyping.

Everything in Willette's paintings reveals the lithographer. Full of feeling, like Gavarni, and equally interested in woman, impulsive, gay, a mild egoist, he established himself between heaven and earth, in an attic on the hill of Montmartre, where he set about creating in his own image a child-like and charming

LOVIS CORINTH. *The Rape.* Etching

world, full of allegories, dreams, good fairies and bogeys.   He gave new life
to the material of the old romances, and, himself an oddity who blushed at the
mere thought of the nape of a woman's neck or her breasts, succeeded in creating
two new types: the little woman of Montmartre—workgirl, model or grisette,
as improvident as the grasshopper—and the Pierrot of pantomime who is the
twin of his creator.   Willette's lithographs, with their clear greys produced by
little, short, nervous strokes further lightened by the scraper, have a gaiety and
charm all their own.   The drawing in too many of them may be conventional—
a fault of many illustrators—but they have a genuine sensuality and an almost epic
touch that raises their author to minor poet rank among lithographers whose
most successful work has been on a small scale: menus, book covers or vignettes.

Steinlen, whom Willette introduced to the Chat Noir about 1883, experimented with every process in turn. Sustained by the example of Daumier and by a fundamental large-mindedness, he did not take long to abandon anecdotal work and the debauchery of Montmartre. His obsession was the street, with its contrasts, perspectives, lights and daily drama. His line, which has the same wide sweep as that of Carrière, seems meant to defend and to protect. When he depicted the sufferings of the people, he hoped, like Anatole France, that he was hastening the coming of better times. He was fond of showing crowds of human beings overshadowed by great symbolic figures. He was also the friend of every stray cat and dog and of all the homeless, and both his etchings and his lithographs show him to be the comrade of the *midinette* in the crowded street and of the tramp shouldering his knapsack. The sincerity he brought to his work enabled him to give his drawing the resolution it had hitherto lacked. His later etchings, with their contrasts and deep bitings, sometimes show less lightness of touch than his lithographs.

Léandre enjoyed using dark greys whose softness contrasts with his deliberate distortions, recalling the enormous heads with which the *Le Charivari* team liked to top minute bodies. It is curious to see how the artist's own feeling can exist side by side with the fatty degeneration from which all his figures seem to suffer.

The vigorous gestures of Jean Véber's cripples, hairdressers, bowls-players and ogres are not easily forgotten. Although he earned his fame by his paintings and colour lithographs, his work in black and white is superior to either. Monochromes like *Public Opinion, Progress, We Carry our Dead,* although less well-known than *The Puller of Teeth* or the *Game of Skill,* show the poetry with which, influenced as he was by Raffet, Goya and Bruegel, he could animate his symbols. These help us to appreciate the epic quality in his little bourgeois scenes, taken from legend or the countryside. The more stupidity he sees around him, the more lyrical Véber becomes. With the courage and violence possessed only by the tender-hearted, he was almost alone at the beginning of the 20th century in bringing his distorting gaze unhesitatingly to bear on social and political life, and in denouncing the masses for either allowing themselves to be kept under by brutes or demagogues, or else devouring their masters.

The impulse given to lithography by Toulouse-Lautrec and Forain induced several other talented artists, who felt their influence to a greater or lesser degree, among others Hermann Paul, Ibels, Abel Faivre and Neumont, to follow their example. A little later, another child of the Butte, Poulbot, the adopted son of Willette, recreated the clown type and showed the narrow, steep streets peopled with little men brought down to scale—a whole new poetry of asphalt.

PIERRE BONNARD. *Child in Lamplight.* *1896.* Colour lithograph

PAUL GAUGUIN. *Nave, Nave Fenua.* *c. 1895.* Coloured Woodcut

It was largely due to French influence that the work of painter-engravers came back into favour in Europe. It was to Paris that etchers, lithographers and line engravers from every country came for intellectual and technical guidance, in reaction against the outworn formulas still taught in most of the schools.

The diverse tendencies in Germany, ranging from crude realism to dreams and symbols, are exemplified by the poetry of Max Klinger (1856-1920) and the penetration shown by Leibl in his family scenes, the portraits of the Berliner Stauffer-Bern (1857-1891) and the country scenes of Fritz Boehle. The Impressionist influence is apparent in the work of Max Liebermann (1847-1935), as gifted as he was easily influenced. After long stays in France, he came home to tackle every style and every type of theme (portraits, equestrian scenes, nudes, to name only some) with enthusiasm and success. Apart from him, Corinth, in both his copperplates and his lithographs, is the one who comes nearest, by his links with Paris, to what was later to be known as the Paris School.

Slevogt was also an etcher and lithographer of most varied talent with a brilliant imagination. To the Norwegian Edward Munch (1863-1944) we owe the *Mortuary* and some large and powerful lithograph portraits including those of Strindberg, Ibsen and Mallarmé. Munch was also known for his woodcuts, a technique that seemed to suit an expressionist artist who had a dramatic force that sometimes recalls Vallotton.

At the same time, in England, Ricketts and Nicholson were also using wood as a medium. Belgian art was chiefly famous at this time for its illustrators—Max Elskamp, painter and poet, Mime, Tielmans, Cosyns and Pellens—while the Flemish genius and its contrasts were represented by the occasionally somewhat crude etchings of Bertsoen, Laermans and Knopff.

The English school of engraving has always laid great stress on the quality of the execution and the art of biting. Legros' influence is obvious in the robust portraits on copperplate of Osborne and Augustus John. Muirhead Bone's best work was in landscape, which he freed from the excessive minuteness of Griggs. Lithography attracted new adherents in Sickert, the friend of Whistler and Degas, Shannon, Rothenstein and Conder who produced much successful work, of which the most elegant and vigorous examples are to be found in the field of portraiture.

In Holland, Pieter Dupont (1870-1911), bravely refusing to allow himself to be carried away by momentary fashion though faithful to his own period, used pure line engraving to produce forceful and deeply felt pictures of country scenes, which reveal his sympathy with animals such as farm horses and plough oxen. He regarded etching as a degenerate art and himself turned back to Dürer. He produced a number of powerful portraits, that of Steinlen for example, and was almost the only precursor of the revival of line engraving for which the young 20th-century engravers were to be responsible, by demonstrating that its rigid lines could be used equally well for new art forms like cubism.

Lovis Corinth. *Girl in a Bodice. 1892.* Etching

KATHE KOLLWITZ. *Self-portrait.* *1893.* Etching and aquatint

WOOD ENGRAVING FROM 1860 TO 1900

Gustave Doré (1832-1883) began at the age of seventeen by producing lithographs of current events and one or two portfolios of satiric drawings, including
Parisian Menagerie. He was inspired in turn by the English caricaturists, Traviès,
Töpffer and Daumier, but lost little time in discovering that his true vocation
was for illustration. He possessed great facility and overpowering imagination,
and was ready to undertake anything. No publisher ever had a quicker or more
compliant collaborator. 'If', said Théophile Gautier, 'a publisher were to ask

him to illustrate the influence of the flea on woman's emotions, I feel sure he would find a means of doing it.' He was an indefatigable worker and more than ten thousand of his wood engravings have been catalogued. With equal liveliness and assurance, he passed from Balzac to Dante, from Cervantes to Shakespeare.

His gifts as a reporter and storyteller never failed him and brought him long periods of collaboration with such publications as the *Monde Illustré* and the *Tour du Monde*. While Daumier always found it difficult to make a living and died in poverty, Doré, by the age of thirty-eight, had already amassed over seven million francs.

The speed with which he worked made it necessary for him to leave the reproduction of his drawings to others and he quickly discovered that they gained in power when they were engraved on wood. After one or two failures, he found

KÄTHE KOLLWITZ. *Scene from Germinal.* *c. 1895.* Etching

EDVARD MUNCH. *Portrait of Mallarmé.* *1896.* Lithograph

PIETER DUPONT. *Portrait of Steinlen.* *1901.* Line engraving

GUSTAVE DORÉ. *The Wandering Jew. 1856.* Woodcut

in Pisan, Lavieille and Dumont a trio capable of carrying out his intentions to perfection and even of giving the hasty indications jotted down for them a character that they would probably not have had if Doré had engraved them himself. The three had already shown their skill when reproducing book vignettes, in the brilliancy they managed to give to the reserved spaces within the sharp outlines.

Unhappily, in Doré's time publishers and the public preferred works on a much larger scale. Repressing the painter and perhaps even the sculptor in him, carried along by his success and by fresh ambitions, Doré's views became progressively larger. When doing the illustrations for the *Contes Drolatiques* which were exactly suited to his genius and remain his masterpiece, he was completely at his ease; when it came to filling in all the blank spaces of a folio volume against time, his inspiration failed him and he lost himself in a morass of detail, forgetting the composition as a whole. The plates he produced then may be picturesque, but being overweighted they tire the eye. Some of his lithographs, such as *Dante and Virgil* or the *Rue de la Vieille-Lanterne*, are genuinely inspired, but he took to relying too much on his powers of presentation and achieving a quick

Félix Vallotton. *The Bargain. c. 1891.* Woodcut

effect, and on his own scintillating gaiety, and began to draw from memory without troubling to study his subjects. This might be forgiven him when it was a case of books like *Pantagruel* or *Voyage aux Pyrénées,* but not when it came to the Bible, Dante, Shakespeare or Cervantes which, alone of Doré's contemporaries, a Delacroix or a Daumier were fit to illustrate. He made no distinction between one author and another, and continued throughout to employ the same conventional backgrounds, the same contrasts, the same gestures. Gustave Geffroy has rightly pointed out the way in which he tried to make up for these deficiencies by exaggerating his line and movements.

Even more serious, however, were the expedients adopted by his interpreters. Imagining themselves on a level with artists, their misuse of tone by which they thought to enrich wood engraving rapidly brought about the decline of the art. Raymond Boyer has summed up the dangers in an article in *L'Image:* 'How is it that line has been imperceptibly ousted from its position in favour of tone? However it has come about, Porret's exact reproductions of the line of the drawing, which were an ornament to any book, are now having to give away to more ambitious interpretations which make use of ink wash and stump-work in a sly attempt to increase their own importance. The men who do the engraving are taking too much upon themselves and the art of engraving is changing. Wood, that formerly innocent medium, is being subjected to all the latest refinements as though it were a plate being bitten.'

Printers like Rouget, Lavieille or Lavoignat had faithfully carried out the instructions that artists like Daumier, Gavarni or Raffet would themselves write on the block. But Doré's interpreters, highly-skilled technicians like Pisan, Pannemaker, Gusman and Perrichon, would embroider his work, like actors of the Italian Comedy. Burty wrote in 1864, à propos of *Don Quixote:* 'It is not contemporary engravers we complain of, so much as the methods of certain technical draughtsmen. We know how much talent, originality and skill exists among the modern school of engravers but they are being forced to apply this talent in the wrong way.' In contrast to Doré, Burty instances the charming and lively work of Edmond Morin, the products of whose brilliant imagination, skilfully interpreted by Joliet, appeared in issue after issue of the *Monde Illustré* and showed how, by avoiding excessive contrasts and over-loading, it was pos-sible to achieve the liveliest effects in black and white.

Events only increased the opposition between the views of the artists, who were becoming increasingly unwilling to confide their drawings to the engravers, and the latter who were anxious to find a means of competing with etching and photography. 'What the French School lacks today,' Burty is speaking again, in 1869, 'is not skill so much as audacity.' In the same way, in 1878, we shall find Delaborde comparing Holbein, Geoffroy Tory or Bernard's engravers with the unscrupulous engravers of his own day who, under pretext of im-proving a picture, did not hesitate to carry out experiments entirely contrary to the spirit and technique of wood engraving.

It was not long before they were to take to using a photographic base. 'This putting in the tint by a mechanical process which is the bastard offspring of phot-ography,' wrote Bracquemond, 'takes away from the wood its vigour, accent and whole character. Instead of the engraver using the crispness and precision of his incisions to vary and draw attention to the values, and to bring the picture into harmony with the text, it becomes increasingly apparent that there has been a complete divorce not only between the original design and its interpretation, but also between text and ornamentation.'

Almost the only artists to rebel against the deplorable influence of Doré were Morin and Daniel Vierge, in whose work sensitive drawing links a sense of drama to a sense of light. Vierge *anticipated* the work of the engraver and gave back its meaning to the word 'actualité'. He also opened the way to an excep-tional artist in Auguste Lepère, who had begun as an interpreter of other men's work. In him, for the first time for centuries, wood engraving found a craftsman who was also an artist, a technician who could interpret his own work.

Accustomed from the age of fifteen to working in wood, Lepère became a regular contributor to the *Monde Illustré,* alongside Langeval, Martin, Tony Beltrand, Florian and Paillard. The first wood engraving to his own design dates from 1876, but it was only after 1886 that he began to concentrate on original work *(Rue de la Montagne Sainte-Geneviève, The Seine at the Pont d'Austerlitz).* Soon afterwards he gave up accepting commissions for the press, which were little better than hard labour, in order to confine his work to reproducing what he himself had felt or seen.

Up to that time, the staff of the *Monde Illustré* or the English or American magazines had merely to make hurried reproductions either of second rate drawings (always excepting those of Constantin Guys) or of photographs printed directly on to specially prepared woodblocks. Large blocks would be cut into eight or twelve pieces and shared out among the engravers, and later put together again. Often they had to interpret pictures of which they had never seen the original —copies of copies—without having time to worry about either forms or outlines or what it was necessary to leave out, everything being subjected to the same network of lines.

The admiration with which Bracquemond regarded the work produced by Lepère from about 1881 onwards certainly hastened the latter's development. In a work *(Trois Livres)* published some years later which, despite its small size, contains perhaps more truths about engraving and the art of illustration than had ever been collected before, Bracquemond described the essential elements that make up the beauty of a wood engraving.

'A print', he writes, 'should carry with it the mark of what it is. There should be no attempt at hiding the process by which it was made; a lithograph should be obviously a lithograph and a wood engraving a wood engraving...The value of a drawing, lithograph or wood engraving lies in the amount of modelling it contains. What I ask of a wood engraving, then, is crisp white lines with good blacks in between...The present incapacity for leaving any white surface on the paper untouched is one of the symptoms of the present sick state of modern art. Contrary to the opinion of certain collectors and most artists, I say that it is not black which is the basic element in a print, but the white of the paper. Like the light it represents, it is the white of the paper that provides the feeling and movement.'

Lepère said once: 'It may well be that my originality simply consists in being as little original as possible; in avoiding virtuosity, and merely following the directions I give myself when designing my engravings.' He worked always from the complex to the simple and, in his light composition, eliminates every secondary or transitory value that might detract from the essential picture. The logical conclusion of this was to give up working against the natural grain of the wood which made it as smooth and unyielding as copper, and take to using wood cut along the grain which a child could easily engrave with a small knife. Even so, the main difference does not consist in substituting a softer for a harder material—even with wood cut against the grain there is no need for anything but the simplest indications, as can be see from the work of all Berwick's predecessors—but in the spirit which was to be brought to wood engraving in the future, whichever way the wood was cut.

Lepère later came to be admired chiefly for the simplification which produced his striking contrasts and warm flat surfaces, and his elimination of half-tones, but this should not make us forget wherein his real superiority as an engraver lay. With the vast resources at his command and as though intoxicated at being his own interpreter, he made the fullest use of his gifts as reporter and artist in his contributions to *Harpers Magazine, Black and White,* the *Revue Illustrée* and *L'Illustration. Rue de la Montagne Sainte-Geneviève* (1887), *Rouen Cathedral* (1888) and *Paris under Snow* (1890) are true masterpieces to which this Parisian, who had inherited so much from the 18th century, has devoted all his vigorous and lively talent and his sense of movement and values.

Lepère beat down the prejudices of publishers as well as bibliophiles, who still refused to hear of a book being decorated with anything but etching, often of a most deplorable kind, and carried the engravers with him in his attempt to revive the art of illustration. He encouraged the younger generation of artists to imitate him: Lucien Pissarro, the sons of Tony Beltrand, J.-E. Laboureur. By the kind of natural reaction that is the life of all art, engravers were coming to abandon the minute work of the *'similistes'* for a synthesis of which only popular art, the unconscious guardian of tradition, had preserved the freshness. The word *'naïveté'* recovered a power of attraction that the word *'savoir'* had lost. The catchword in all the studios now was *synthesis.* Almost at the same time, Gauguin, Armand Seguin, Maurice Denis and Aristide Maillol all turned back to the earliest of all the engraving processes. A true precursor of the movement was Emile Bernard, who had founded *Le Bois* as early as 1888. He printed this paper himself, and its moving little 'pictures', some of which he touched up by hand, have the ingenuousness of the holy pictures sold by travelling salesmen. In addition to the professionals, various painters who had only recently come to engraving, and even some writers like Rémy de Gourmont, the founder of *L'Imagier,* and Alfred Jarry, created an unexpectedly variegated school of wood engraving. One after the other, under the undoubted influence of Emile Bernard and Vallotton, Maurice Delcourt, Alexandre Charpentier, Luce, Bottini, Paul-Emile Colin, Vibert, Ardail, Nicholson, Laboureur, Huard, Jeanniot, d'Espagnat and Jossot popularised the type of engraving in which deeply incised lines enable heavily inked surfaces, whether flat or contoured, to be contrasted directly with the light surfaces.

Next came the turn of colour. Artists like Henri Rivière, Guérard, Tony Beltrand and Lucien Pissarro, and also Beltrand's sons to whom he had handed on his sense of ornament as well as the art of colouring inks, remembered the added attraction of polychrome prints. Lepère, profiting from his study of Ugo da Carpi's chiaroscuro woodcuts as well as of eastern prints, produced his *Time for Tea* in which can be discerned already a promise of the richness of the *Corpus Christi Procession at Nantes* and the fine printing of *A Rebours.* The lesson he never ceased to drive home was that the text and the illustrations must form a whole, and he successfully demonstrated the superiority of wood engraving for book illustrations by the publication of *Nantes* in 1900, followed by *La Bièvre, Les Gobelins, Saint-Séverin, A Rebours, Fairs and Markets in Normandy,* thus confounding at one stroke the prejudices of the bibliophiles. Under his direction, and that of Tony Beltrand and Roger-Marx, *L'Image,* which was founded in 1896, formed a rallying point for wood engravers, brought in new recruits like Laboureur, and defended the rights of both original and reproductive wood engraving. Lepère was also instrumental in organising the great 1902 exhibition at the *Ecole des Beaux-Arts* entitled *Cinq siècles de Gravure sur bois,* and in creating, in the place of the earlier *Société des Artists de la Gravure sur bois,* the *Société de la Gravure sur bois originale,* 'founded with the object of preserving the true process of printed wood engraving, in black and white or colour, by holding exhibitions of the works of engravers and promoting the art by means of publications, lectures and retrospective exhibitions.'

This revival was to be successful also outside the world of book illustration. Jacques Beltrand, whose first colour-wash wood engravings appeared in *L'Almanach* in 1897 and who showed great technical skill and knowledge allied with a nobility of inspiration drawn from the best work of the past, brought back the large decorative print and the tint-drawing *(Faun playing the Flute, The Labourer, The Old Tree, River and Trees).* The vigour and delicacy of the impression no less than the intelligence and imaginative gift for ornament shown in his translation of certain works (including Maurice Denis' *Fioretti* and *Vita Nuova,* the final version of which is due to him), show that he was more than a mere interpreter.

Henri Rivière was obsessed by Japanese art, which had influenced so many painters during the previous five-and-twenty years—curiously enough without European wood engraving having profited in the least by the lessons that art could have taught it. He now came back again to the skilled and delicate art of colour-washed wood engraving. It was in this that he achieved his greatest successes, although he was attracted by several other types of technique, including etching and lithography. The admiration for Hokusai and Hiroshige which led him to imitate the very shape of their prints and type of signature, also led him to re-discover their seemingly inimitable subtle harmonies and skilful diminutions of light and shade. In his prints Brittany appears like some island in the Japanese archipelago. His powers of sympathetic observation prevented his admiration for Japanese art from fettering that freedom of invention which Gauguin retained before a Maori drawing, or Picasso before a wooden negro carving. By using powdered colours mixed with water he was able to obtain a density of tone, and also a transparency and a freshness unobtainable with aniline colours. Rivière was his own printer and skilfully managed to obtain charming effects, which many French and English engravers tried to imitate. Even some sculptors, such as Charpentier, Carabin and Pierre Roche, tried in imitation of the Japanese to revive the art of embossing wood or plaster; while Lucien Pissarro, in collaboration with his wife, produced a number of chiaroscuro woodcuts after his father's drawings and entitled *Work in the Fields,* as well as a whole series of delightful little illustrations for works published by the Eragny Press in 1894 and the years following.

Gauguin was a sculptor in wood before he became an engraver, which makes his earliest wood engraving (1894), inspired by his memories of Tahiti, later than his lithographs. The latter had taught him the use of glass paper and light erasing, which he remembered when he came to wood engraving, in which very light lines cut with a fine needle contrast with deep lines dug out by the gouge. Here too we see that mixture of subtlety and violence so characteristic of him. Marcel Guérin tells us that he printed his engravings himself, without a press and often without a roller, all he needed being a very light coating of ink. The irregularity of the pressure produces unexpected modulations and semitones that contrast with the great unfilled spaces and the absolute blacks. The early states often look like spoiled proofs until, as one state follows another, the formless greys are touched up with stronger tones and the linear pattern is strengthened. In some of the engravings colour has been added by means of an additional block.

Gauguin's second stay in Tahiti (1895-1903) produced a number of new compositions, some of which he later changed into bas-reliefs. 'I am sending you', he wrote to Daniel de Monfreid in 1899, 'a set of engravings I have done on rather inferior wood, with my eyesight giving me more and more trouble. They cannot help being different from the daily grind of my usual work and they are full of faults, but, I think, very interesting as art.' 'It is just because it represents a return to primitive times', he adds further on, 'that this engraving is interesting; wood engraving as used for illustrations is daily becoming more sickening, like photogravure. I am sure that within a reasonable time my engravings, which are so different from what is being done nowadays, will have become really valuable.' Hence Gauguin, by a different route, had reached the same conclusions as Lepère. Being unable to sell the prints, Monfreid gave them away to Maurice Denis and Maillol. Some of the latter's engravings, *Women on the Beach* for instance, clearly show Gauguin's influence. Later, Maillol was to adopt the black-line method by which to stress his contours.

Typographical ornament plays an important part in many of Gauguin's engravings (for example, the title pages of *Sourire*), which contain potentially all that we find in André Derain's early work. Gauguin's models were the Aztec sculptures he had seen at the 1889 exhibition, Persian, Cambodian and Egyptian art. 'The great mistake', he once wrote, 'was Greek art, no matter how beautiful it was.'

Gauguin's work was exceptional and technically isolated. In some places the contours are marked by black lines, in others by the whites. In his composition, the proportions of his figures and the distribution of light, he shows the greatest individuality and very little care for convention. He often uses a black reserved surface to express a light tone, while his whites, produced by the use of the gouge or of glass paper, are exaggerated to suggest shadow. Sometimes his figures stand out in black against a light background, sometimes the opposite *(Love and be Happy)*. In the wood engravings done during his second Tahiti period, there

237

seem fewer of the fine lines drawn with the point; they are closer to lithographs or the earliest Western wood engravings and popular drawings. A picture like *The Turkey-cock*, for instance, anticipates Dufy's *Bestiary*. But, apart from this, Gauguin's art, at once violent and endearing, cannot be compared to any other. Gauguin was destined to follow Emile Bernard in exercising upon numerous painter-engravers an influence parallel to that of Lepère and Vallotton.

WOOD ENGRAVING IN ENGLAND AND GERMANY

It would be wrong to under-estimate the influence of the simultaneous attempts being made in England and Germany to restore wood engraving to its former freedom. In engraving as in painting, a return to the past is not without its dangers. It is not easy to retrace one's steps back through the centuries, and to try to be simple almost always means ceasing to be so. But both in Germany, under the influence of Overbeck and the Nazarene movement, and in England, under that of Burne Jones and the Pre-Raphaelites, it was in all good faith and often in all innocence that painters, tired of the falsity and tasteless elaboration taught in the schools, endeavoured to turn back to purer sources of inspiration. Their idealism was genuine, although no doubt, as a theory, Pre-Raphaelitism was full of holes.

Fuseli, English by adoption, and a visionary who, like Blake, lacked only a surer sense of form, was already being reproached for being 'literary', a criticism also levelled against Turner, especially in the latter part of his life. But it is undeniable that the English school of painters have often found wood a better medium of expression than canvas, for the very reason that wood, by definition a primitive material, calls for simple treatment even by artists with a complicated, not to say decadent approach.

Like Blake and Fuseli, Calvert and Richmond often confused art and literature. The few wood engravings done in 1857 by Dante Gabriel Rossetti as illustrations for some poems of Tennyson—another of whose illustrators was John Everett Millais—as well as his incidental illustrations of the early Italian poets, done in 1861, show him to have studied the woodcuts of the 15th century as well as the intaglio work of Drevet and Mantegna, whose taste for long draperies that emphasise the bodies beneath, he shared.

Arthur Boyd, Houghton, Millais, Pinwell and Sandys were others who used wood for illustrating a number of books, including the *Arabian Nights, Christ's Parables* (1864) and *Don Quixote*. But war was not really declared on colour until the second wave of Pre-Raphaelites and the teaching of William Morris, poet, aesthete and engraver. With William Crane, he founded the Kelmscott Press, that turned out so many attractive editions of Chaucer, Shakespeare, Keats and Rossetti, illustrated by Crane and Burne Jones, between 1891 and 1896. From then onwards, wood engravings were appreciated above all for their ornamental value and looked on as actually forming part of the text— to such an extent that it was sometimes enclosed in an engraved border and pages were scattered with dream-like creatures playing among trees and flowers, a trifle stiff and symbolic according to the taste of the time, and their grace rather too stylised.

The work of William Morris and the Kelmscott Press was carried on by the Dial Press, founded by Hacon and Ricketts, and by the fine editions issued by Lucien Pissarro towards the end of the century under the imprint of the Eragny Press.

In Germany—following the views inculcated by Overbeck and his followers—Friedrich, M. von Schwind and, above all, Rethel *(The Dance of Death)* went back to Holbein and Dürer to find inspiration for their wood engraving. In a similar search for simplification, Joseph Sattler (1867-1931) turned to the woodcuts of the 15th century.

INTO THE TWENTIETH CENTURY

The 19th century was marked, especially in France, by a revival of engraving techniques of all kinds and their final emancipation from many of the hitherto accepted conventions. No other period boasts so many masterpieces in this medium and at no other period have artists responded with greater enthusiasm to the lure of black and white. Formerly, a print had been judged by the degree of 'finish' it showed; by the number of lines appearing on the plate. Line engraving had remained a perennial favourite, both with artists and public who admired it for the amount of work it entailed. A much higher place had been accorded to reproductive than to original engraving and, despite the popularity of Dürer and Rembrandt, the engraved work of other masters such as Callot, Claude, Piranesi or Canaletto was very little sought-after.

During the 19th century, however, the cause of 'free engraving' was taken up by many of the foremost artists and connoisseurs, until today, thanks to be improvements in mechanical photographic processes, it is probably destined to oust reproductive engraving altogether. A growing number of artists discovered, in due course, that ink and paper could be used to convey the subtlest suggestions, and that the beauty of their compositions could actually be enchanced by the transpositions and sacrifices required by this medium. Writers like Baudelaire, Burty, Delaborde and Roger-Marx, as well as Manet, Bracquemond, Degas, Whistler, Odilon Redon, Pissarro and Toulouse-Lautrec among the artists, all contributed towards freeing engraving from the conventions that had grown up round it during the centuries, partly owing to the influence of the technical engravers who, being more or less devoid themselves of artistic inspiration, contemptuously dismissed as mere 'prentice hands' the very men who were to give a whole new impulse to the art.

Before Goya, portrait engraving had been the most popular form; but from his time onwards this was gradually replaced by landscape (hitherto the preserve of Rembrandt, Claude, Canaletto and Piranesi), nudes, and real or imaginary conversation pieces. The artist-engravers, with their variety of themes drawn from their imagination or the realities of daily life, refused to be daunted by the length of time needed for the actual execution. They realised that an engraving, like a picture, must be a synthesis.

Odilon Redon has left a record of his fights with his printers who considered nothing worthy of admiration but 'fine grain', and who agreed with the professional teachers of engraving in denouncing his lithographs as monstrosities. In wood engraving, Lepère advocated the use of clear-cut lines and introduced the use of wood blocks cut with, instead of against, the grain. Subsequently, Gauguin turned for fresh inspiration to the primitive civilisations still at that time considered as barbarian. Bracquemond's dictum on the incessant practice needed to achieve freedom of execution has already been mentioned and Burty also emphasised that technical skill could never be more than a necessary adjunct to the development of an artist's inherent qualities. Painters like Whistler, Degas, Pissarro, Toulouse-Lautrec or Vuillard were fully alive to all the resources of their craft. Convinced as they were, however, that in art simplification is a greater aid to progress than amplification, it was only long after their deaths that their theories triumphed over the resistance offered to them by the professional engravers, print-sellers and collectors.

It must be acknowledged, nevertheless, that the search for freedom carried with it a certain degree of risk. As early as 1862, in *Le Boulevard*, Baudelaire's almost infallible intuition led him, as we have already seen, to utter a warning against the danger to engraving likely to be represented by the crowd of its untaught or superficial practitioners, with their carelessness, lack of precision and weak or ignorant execution. By the beginning of the 20th century, too many artists were regarding wood or stone plates merely as contrivances for multiplying copies of a composition. Desirous simply of following the fashion, they used copper or stone indifferently, never stopping to consider which material would best serve their individual gifts. Their rapidly executed woodcuts have none of the zest or mystery that distinguish those of Gauguin, and are as dull and finicky as the work produced by Doré's interpreters. In lithography, all direct contact with the stone came to be lost through the general use of transfer paper. Etching was reduced to the mere reproduction of drawings done after pictures, without any consideration being given to the time needed for biting or to the need for more than one state; in other words, the need to proceed by stages. Work was more and more hastily done and increasing reliance placed on the pressmen and printers and their various resources. The day may even come when artists, while still claiming to do creative work, will simply hand over a drawing, water-colour or, the last infamy, a canvas to be reproduced in facsimile, the result to be signed and numbered and sold for an original print.

But perhaps this is to paint too dark a picture. After a break at the beginning of the 20th century, due to the discouragement felt by the older artists at the indifference of the public, the art of original engraving found new adherents, and wood-engraving, etching and lithography all came back into favour. Toulouse-Lautrec, Bonnard and Vuillard were followed by Rouault, Naudin, Picasso, Vlaminck, Maillol, Marquet, Matisse, Jacques Villon, Dunoyer de Segonzac, Dufy, Frélaut, Marie Laurencin, Charles Dufresne, Pascin, Laprade, Laboureur, Gromaire, and many others. These infused new life into the indefatigable Société des Peintres-Graveurs and, after them, other groups such as the Peintres-Graveurs Indépendants also helped to popularize original engraving. Even the unorthodox movements like Cubism and its by-product Abstract Art have produced a number of unexpected and interesting results.

But among the riot of engraving that has appeared during the present century, the only artists who will survive are those who have a higher ambition than merely to follow contemporary fashion, and who can show that they have their own inevitable and individual style, their own original vision of the material and spiritual worlds. They are the only ones worthy to be considered legitimate descendants in the line of Dürer, Rembrandt, Goya, Géricault, Daumier, Redon and Toulouse-Lautrec. In painting, ingenuity can sometimes create the illusion of talent; but not in the more austere realm of black and white. This deserves to be remembered today when public taste seems to be fascintaed by the colour which most of the earlier painter-engravers were wise enough to eschew, and when the print has abandoned its former modesty and discretion.

This book, which began with an expression of faith, ends with the expression of a hope that the print, alive to both its potentialities and its imitations, may always remain faithful to the real cause of its being.

LIST OF ILLUSTRATIONS

Numbers in italics refer to colour plates

243

245

INDEX OF NAMES